THINKING MUSICALLY

ANUPAMA PATTABIRAMAN & URI BRAM

Capara Books

THINKING MUSICALLY

Capara Books

1st Edition

Text Copyright © Anupama Pattabiraman & Uri Bram
Cover Copyright © Natalie Harney
Design Copyright © Matt Jeppesen

All rights reserved.

*to the Bogotá-Catskills Collective,
who always lead us home.*

Contents

INTRODUCTION ... i
Pitch ... 1
Scales ... 45
Harmony ... 77
Rhythm & Beat ... 111
Coda ... 131

INTRODUCTION

You walk into a café one day and hear a conversation in a beautiful language that you don't understand. It sounds like a babbling brook, or the singing of birds. It makes you feel happy, sad, big and small.

For many of us, this is music: we appreciate its beauty, but it's a language we don't understand.

After weeks or months of hearing people speak this language you decide you can't take it any more: you simply must learn how to speak it. Maybe a teacher comes over and teaches you some vocabulary, then some sentences, then how to read this language so you can read some of the very great books this language has to offer. Perhaps after many years you can speak beautiful passages in this language, and appreciate your listening to it all the more.

And yet... you feel that there's something missing. Like children learn languages by repetition and practice, we can certainly learn how to make beautiful music just by copying things we like and slowly learning to make creations of our own. But there is more to music: there are rules of "grammar" and "syntax," if you will, that explain a lot of how music works. In fact, the rules behind music are perhaps more beautiful, more consistent, and more enlightening than the rules of grammar: there are incredible mathematical patterns and regularities behind the way that music works. But for better or worse, few of us outside of the music academies learn these secrets behind the wonderful world of music.

Now, learning Spanish grammar won't let you write poems like Pablo Neruda, and (what's more) the most beautiful, staggering, delightful elements of any great use of language tend to be exactly the parts we can't explain or quantify. And yet, understanding those rules can still give us a lot of satisfaction, and possibly use — whether through giving us a basis for our creative pursuits, or simply to satisfy the unending hunger of human curiosity. And that's what we hope to do in this book: make music a slightly less foreign language, through understanding how music truly works. We hope you will enjoy reading this as much as we enjoyed writing it.

Pitch

What is music? You already know what music is in an "I know it when I hear it" way. When your favorite song gets played on the radio, that is music. When someone whispers "I love you," that is not (except metaphorically). When an orchestra strikes up a tune, that is music. When a car accelerates on a roadway, that is not.

There is a gray area, to be sure, and we don't mean thrash metal. We might not think of the sound of a trash can being put down on a sidewalk as music, yet there are groups (like the talented object-bangers *Stomp*) who have turned such noises into very interesting percussive compositions. As another example, the contemporary composer John Cage composed a piece called 4'33", consisting of four minutes and thirty-three seconds of silence. Can we call this music? The answer is up for grabs. But as interesting as these questions are, they're well outside the purpose of this book: to better understand the fascinating world of the well-defined music we listen to everyday.

What separates music from everyday noise is that it's a particular set of soundwaves that seem harmonious to our ears, make us sway our hips to a beat, and — somehow — wield the power to make us feel elated, angry, or sad. Put on your dancing shoes, your singing hat, and any other literal or metaphorical attire you might deem necessary, and let's get started.

She Bangs The Drums

Music consists of sounds. How does sound happen, physically speaking? Generally, we hear sound when an object vibrates, which sets off vibrations in the air around it, which sets off vibrations in our eardrums. When these vibrations enter our eardrums, our ears send signals to our brain that give us the sensation of hearing. It is also possible for sound to reach us through solid objects, and in fact it is also possible for sound to reach us through our teeth instead of our eardrums — after Beethoven went deaf he would hold a wooden stick between his teeth and press it to his piano keys if he needed to hear a note. In that case the sound travelled up the stick, through his teeth, inside his skull, and into his magnificent musical brain. One way or another, though, our perception of sound is always caused by a chain of vibrations.

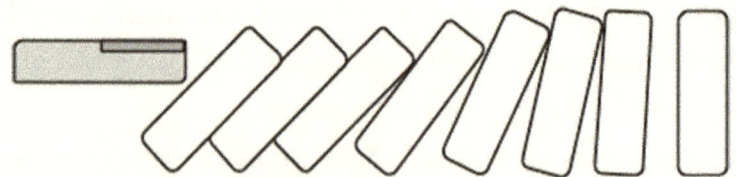

To understand how the vibration-chain works, think about a row of dominos. If you knock down the first one, it will cause the rest to fall sequentially until you reach the end of the row.

Similarly with soundwaves, when you hit a drum (for example), the vibration of the drum-skin sets off the vibration of the nearest air-molecules, which sets off the vibration in *their* nearest air-molecules, and onwards like a chain of dominos. Eventually the air-vibrations reach air-molecules right next to your eardrum, which sets off the vibration in your eardrum itself, which causes messages to be sent to your brain that cause you to perceive a sound. Simple as that!

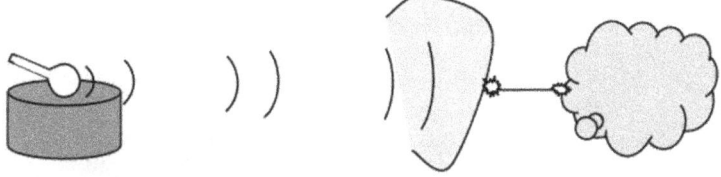

from the drum... through the air... to your ear-drum... to the brain!

When you think of all the common ways to make noises, this physical explanation of sound makes sense. Hitting things, plucking things, blowing things, and dropping things onto other things are all common ways to create musical instruments (though unfortunately no orchestra is irreverent enough to name its sections this way). Each of those techniques fundamentally involves making a solid object vibrate to set off a chain of vibrations that runs through the air and arrives at our eardrums. So far so good.

Now, sound travels as a wave. This is the easiest way to imagine what a wave looks like, even if it's not 100% physically accurate:

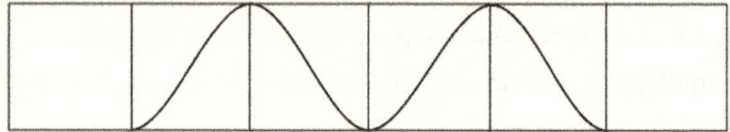

When a particular object makes a sound, the waves emanate outwards from it in all directions — like a circle of waves emanating from a stone dropped in a pond. Therefore, if we look at the waves from "on top," the peaks of the waves can be connected with semi-circular arcs like this:

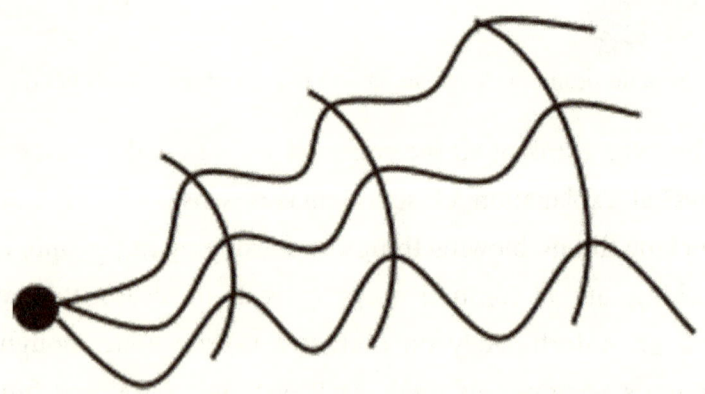

Therefore, for visual convenience, we'll often represent soundwaves by just drawing the arcs that connect the peaks of the waves. Like in the picture we drew of the sound coming out of a drum: those black arcs represent the peaks of a whole bunch of waves that emanate out from the drum and hit our ears:

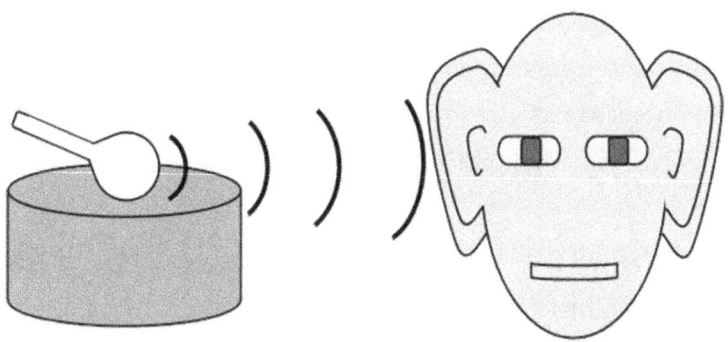

Incidentally, it's quite possible that at some point in your life you've run across the age-old question: if a tree falls in a forest and no-one is there to hear it, does it make a sound? Well, now you know the answer: it certainly still causes vibrations in the air around it, but if there's no ear to hear it, it is never perceived as sound.

Pitch in

We all know that sounds have a property that is described as being "high" or "low": the annoying sound of police sirens is "high," while the throaty drone of a lawnmower engine is "low." What makes one sound "higher" than another? Quite simply, high sounds are generated by objects vibrating faster, low sounds are generated by objects vibrating slower. This is the quality that musicians call **pitch**: the *pitch* of a sound is how high or low we perceive it to be, based on how quickly or slowly the air is vibrating to create that sound in our heads. The musical word pitch even gets a bit of love in colloquial English: when we say that someone has a *high pitched voice*, we simply mean that the person speaks at a high pitch — physically, that the air molecules carrying their voice to us are vibrating unusually quickly.

Graphically, if the wave that produced the sound from the lawnmower engine looked like this:

Then the wave that produced the sound from the police siren might look like this:

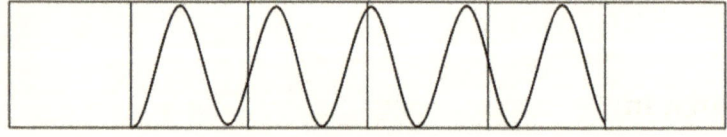

Technically what makes a sound "high pitched" or "low pitched" is how many peaks reach our ear each second: the more peaks that reach us, the higher-pitched the sound is. We call this property **frequency**, because it measures how *frequently* the wave completes a full cycle of movement each second. Imagine one of the waves above moving horizontally from left to right along the screen or page: as soon as one of the peaks has reached the place where the peak in front of it *used* to be when we started, one full cycle has been completed. Frequency is measured in **"Hertz,"** or **Hz** for short, where 1 Hertz means one full cycle per second. If we could hear a wave at 1 Hz (we can't, it's well outside our hearing range), it would have one wave-peak hitting our ear each second. The normal adult hearing range is roughly 20 Hz - 16,000 Hz.

What's the difference between frequency and pitch, then? Well, frequency is an objective physical property of waves that doesn't depend at all on human perception; pitch is a subjective human experience when hearing sounds. The soundwaves created by that famous tree falling in the forest, where nobody hears it, still have a *frequency*, but no-one perceives them to have a *pitch*. In reality, though, the *pitch* we hear is almost entirely determined by the **frequency** of the wave that created it, so the two concepts are incredibly tightly related. We will quantify pitches in Hertz, as well, although technically that should refer to the frequency of the wave that creates a certain pitch in our heads.

When we represent a wave visually, the thing that tells us its pitch is how close together the wave-peaks are — after all, we can't really express the passing of time in a picture. If you imagine the waves on previous pages moving across the screen from left to right at the same speed and eventually hitting our eardrums, the ones where the wave-peaks are very close together will cause more full cycles to reach our ears each second, and the sound they create will therefore be higher-pitched; the ones where the wave-peaks are further apart will cause fewer full cycles to hit our eardrums each second, and the sound they create will therefore be lower-pitched.

Let's move back to the objects that create soundwaves. The simplest way to understand and envisage them is with something like a guitar string: when we pluck the string we can clearly see that it's bouncing up and down very quickly, and that's what pushes the vibrations into the air around it. (On a piano the vibrating strings are "hidden" under the lid, but if we open up a grand piano we can see the strings vibrating there as well). If we plucked a guitar string and watched it vibrate in slow-motion, it might look a little like this:

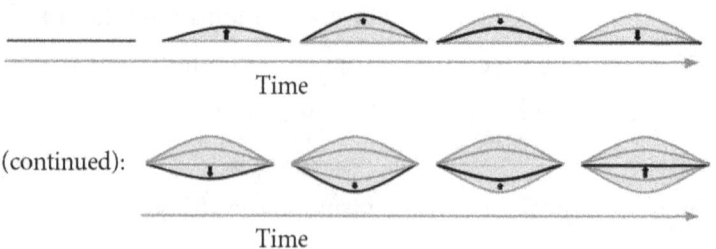

The string goes up and down, up and down, again and again. The amount of time that it takes to go up and down once we call one "oscillation." We could measure, in a second, how many oscillations the string makes: on guitars this tends to be on the order of 100's or 1000's of oscillations per second. For example, the second-lowest string of a properly-tuned acoustic guitar makes 110 oscillations per second. Well spotted, cunning reader—these oscillations per second are exactly the same as frequency. If a guitar string oscillates 110 times each second then the waves it produces will go through 110 cycles every second, and its frequency is 110 Hz. If you have a guitar you can listen along at home — as we said before, 110 Hz is the frequency of the second-lowest string (the *A* string) on a "concert pitch" guitar.

Now, let's say we pluck a different string that's a tad fatter. This one will oscillate more slowly — for example, at a frequency of 82.4 Hz — and we will perceive its pitch to be lower than that of the 110 Hz string. Indeed, 82.4 Hz is the pitch of the bottom *E* string on a normally-tuned guitar; and indeed, the *E* string sounds lower than the *A* string.

You can observe how fatter strings produce lower pitches at home even if you don't have a guitar. Take a thin rubber band, wrap it around an open box, and pluck it. Then place a thicker rubber band next to it. If you pluck both rubber bands, you'll discover that the fatter one sounds lower! This is because fatter strings vibrate more slowly, and so at lower frequencies, than thinner ones. If a friend, parent, or flatmate has just come back from a long night out you may want to go and demonstrate this excellent insight to them; be sure to hold the rubber bands close to their ears and pluck repeatedly. (What, you actually did it? We were kidding. Oh dear).

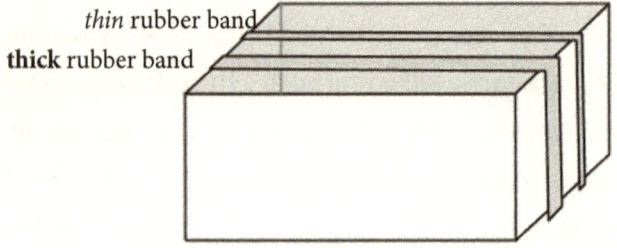

There are several other aspects of a guitar string that affect its frequency. The more *tightly* wound a string is, the higher its pitch will be; hence, guitarists "tune" their instruments by winding their strings tighter to be higher-pitched, or making them looser to lower their pitch, using the big screws (or "pegs") at the top of the instrument. The *length* of a string also affects its pitch, and this is how guitarists manage to create so many wonderful sounds with just six basic strings: by pressing her fingers down at different points along the length of a given string, the guitarist can effectively create a shorter string which will then create a higher-pitched sound. This massively over-dramatised picture shows what happens, although in real life the difference in speed from the vibrations is too small for us to see:

Longer String → Vibrates Slower

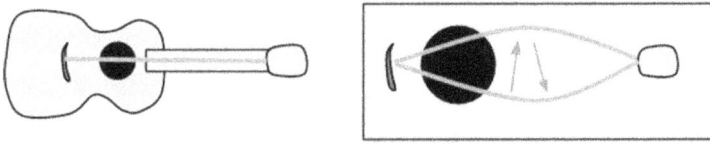

Shorter String → Vibrates Quicker

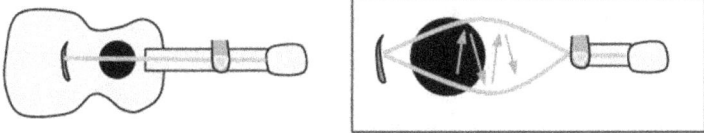

Now, you may wonder: if we pluck a string *harder*, will it vibrate faster and produce a higher pitch? In fact, it won't; the frequency of oscillation of a guitar string is a property of the length, thickness, and tautness of the string, not how hard we pull it. The only effect of plucking the string harder will be to make the sound louder! It's like hitting a xylophone with a mallet: when you strike a xylophone key harder, it doesn't change the pitch of the key, it only makes the sound louder (and more annoying to your neighbors).

Relative Frequencies

Now, we know that some pitches are higher than others, but can we say more than that? Can we compare how far apart — that is, how much higher or lower — one pitch is from another?

One way to do this (in theory) would be to compare absolute difference in frequencies. For example, if your fire alarm beeps at 3000 Hz and mine beeps at 2990 Hz, I could say *the "distance" between our fire alarm beeps is exactly 10 Hz*. In practice, however, this turns out not to be a very useful way to compare pitches. And the reason it's not too useful comes out of a very interesting mathematical phenomenon. It turns out that the way our ears perceive differences between two sounds has nothing to do with the *absolute* difference between their frequencies, and everything to do with the *relative* difference between their frequencies. For example, suppose we play you a pitch at 100 Hz followed by a pitch at 200 Hz, then another one at 400 Hz. Despite the fact that the "gap" is bigger in the second case, your ear will think that the three pitches are spaced "equally far apart"! This is because the relative difference between the frequencies is the same; in each case, the frequency of the second pitch is double the frequency of the first pitch:

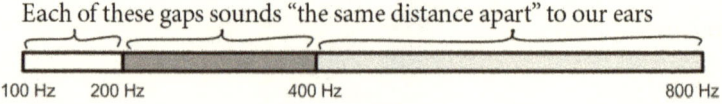

Each of these gaps sounds "the same distance apart" to our ears

An analogy may be useful here. Imagine for a moment that you're running a small but legendary local coffeeshop — let's call it, for example, Yaff's Caff. You need to decide on the sizes of coffee-cup that you're going to offer: some people like less coffee, some people like more coffee, and Yaff's likes to accommodate all of them (though it prefers the caffeine addicts). Now, one option is just to pick some linear increment to increase the cup-sizes by: for example, 4 oz. Maybe the smallest cup would be 12 oz, the medium cup would be 16 oz, the large cup would be 20 oz, and the obscenely large cup would be 24 oz:

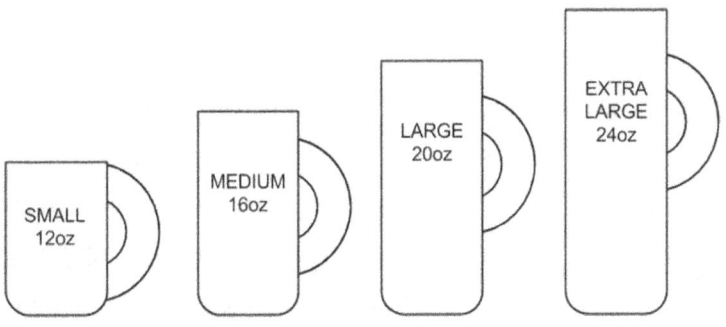

Now, this little system is not without merit, but Yaff's isn't quite happy here: it doesn't necessarily make sense to just have the cup-sizes increase in increments of 4 oz each time. It might make more sense to have larger gaps between the sizes as the cups get larger; this could be true for various reasons, but one example is that fine-grained distinctions might matter more to people when the cups themselves are smaller. Suppose we said "*ok, let's keep the Small at 12 oz but then make every subsequent cup ⅓ larger than the previous one.*" We would come out with something like this:

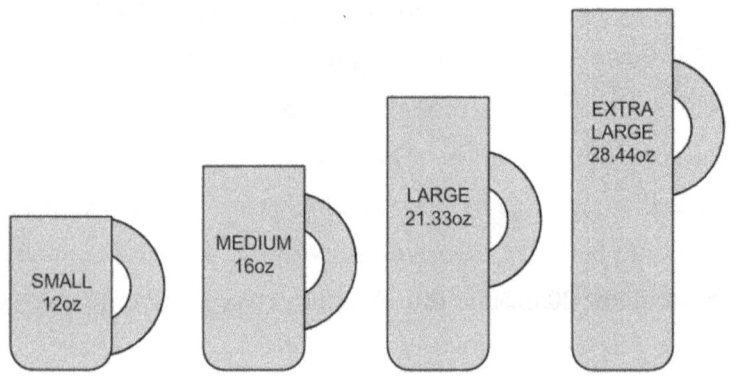

For the first two cups there is actually no difference between the old and new sizes (but only because we chose the numbers for our example that way). As the cups grow, though, the difference becomes quite substantial. And the difference is only going to continue growing: if Yaff's adds a new, larger cup-size under the old system it would be 28 oz, but under the new system it would be almost 38 oz!

Because we perceive sound according to the relative difference in the frequencies, rather than the absolute difference, it makes sense for our musical system to work like the second option; it makes sense for our coffee-cups to be sized relative to each other.

There's something we did in this example which seems so obvious that we didn't even think about it, but which in fact is quite important: we gave every cup-size a *name*, such as "Small" or "Medium" or "Large." Let's think a little about what's going on here. It's clearly possible to have coffee exist in any quantity you can imagine: 10.06 oz, or 22.05 oz, or any other (positive) number whatsoever. But you can't walk into your favourite café and say "I'll have 10.06 oz of your finest brew." Your café decides on a few standard coffee-cup sizes, and you can only order from among that set.

Similarly, it's possible for a pitch to have absolutely any (positive) number as its frequency. However, like at Yaff's Caff, in Western music we have taken a particular set of pitches and given them individual names, and those are the only ones that we commonly use when writing music. Sure, it's possible to bend this rule a little, in the same way that it's possible to go into a café and ask for "a Small, please, but don't fill it up," but in general we only make music from the standard set of pitches. We call these named pitches **notes**.

Since humans are envious creatures, once we have notes we will almost certainly want to compare them. In the same way that the word "distance" describes the amount of space between two points, in music we say that an **interval** is the amount of "space" between two notes. For example, if coffee-cups were notes, we might say that the interval between Medium and Extra Large is two units, or that the interval between Medium and Extra Large is twice the interval between Medium and Large:

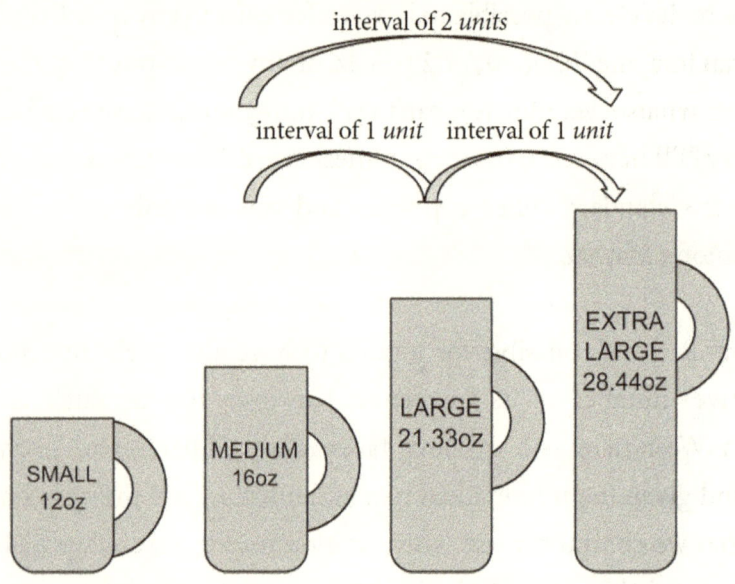

"Now hold your horses there," you may be saying in your head, if you're currently living in the 1800s, "how can you say that the interval between Medium and Large is one unit, and the interval between Large and X-Large is one unit, when one of them is 5.33 oz and the other one is 7.11 oz?"

Here we come to something special and rather wonderful about the kind of mathematical pattern that is based on relative sizes (like our musical notes), rather than absolute sizes. Sure: we could say "the interval between Medium and Large is 5.33 oz, and the interval between Large and X-Large is 7.11 oz," but this doesn't really make a lot of sense for the system we're using — it makes it look like the differences are weird and arbitrary, when in fact there's a very simple number that summarises the differences between the sizes. Every cup in our system is ⅓ larger than the previous cup, so that's the relevant difference, and the unit that we should standardise our measurements around should reflect that. This may take a tiny bit of getting used to but there's really no reason why our units (in general) need to be based on absolute differences, rather than relative differences, and in music it makes most sense to have the second kind. When we talk about an interval of (say) four *units*, we want those units to be based on the relative differences in frequency between the notes, because that's how our brains perceive sound.

The Units of Music

In the same way that money is commonly measured using a big unit (dollars) and a small unit (cents), intervals are commonly measured using "a big unit" and "a small unit" too (there are in fact other units also but they are not really used by everyday musicians). The "big" unit of musical distance is called an **octave**: the interval between a pitch at one frequency and a pitch at twice that frequency. Remember we said that any pitch can be represented as a soundwave that looks (vaguely) like this:

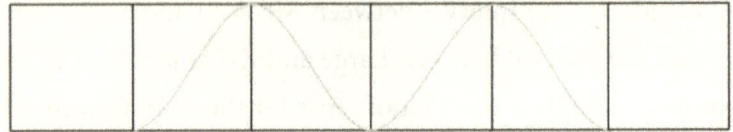

And that a higher-pitched wave would complete more cycles per second, so (in our diagram) its peaks would be closer together.

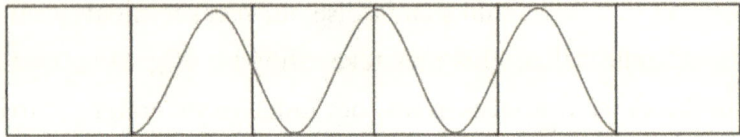

If we keep pushing the wave-peaks closer together, we will soon reach this wave:

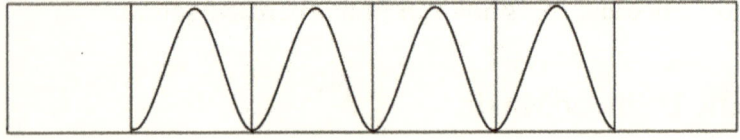

This wave actually has a very special relationship with the grey wave we just looked at: for every one full cycle that the grey wave goes through, this black wave goes through *two* full cycles.

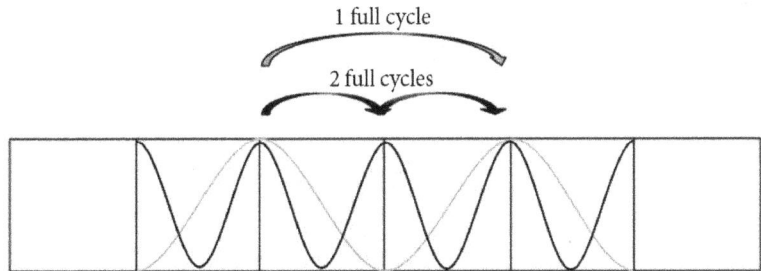

An octave, therefore, is the interval between the pitch of the grey wave and the pitch of the black wave. In terms of their frequencies, that might look something like this:

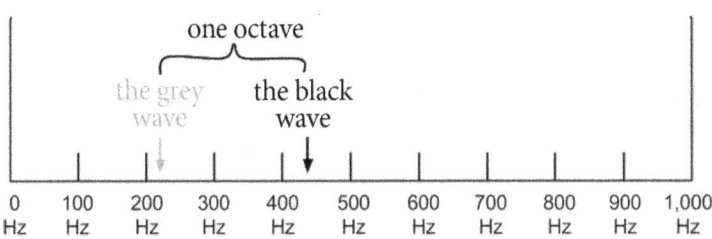

Of course, this effect doesn't simply stop with two waves. If we find another wave that's double the frequency of our black wave:

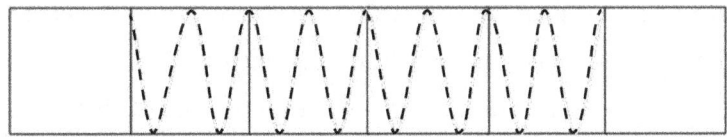

We can put them all together to get something rather overwhelming that looks like this:

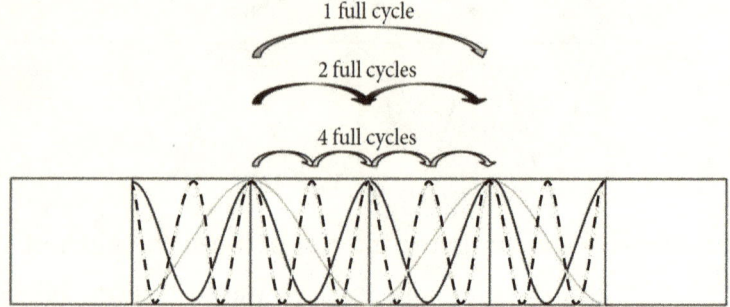

In terms of frequencies again, this combo would now look like this:

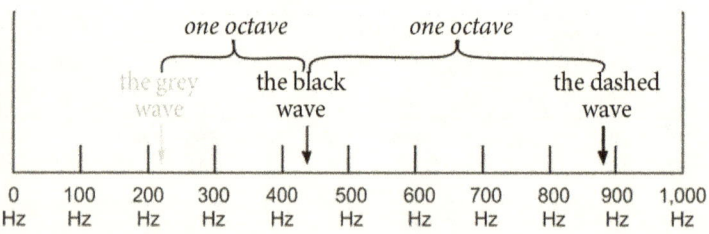

It's blindingly clear that the second octave takes up much more "space" in absolute terms than the first octave. But again, we have to remember that our brains perceive sound in terms of relative frequencies, not absolute frequencies. Since in each case the frequency of the second pitch is exactly twice as high as the frequency of the first pitch, both of those one-octave intervals will sound equally "far apart" to our ears.

The Same Jam

But that's not all: it turns out that the octave actually has some near-magical properties that make it even more exciting than it seemed at first (you were already excited by the octave, right?). Remember that if we overlay the soundwave diagrams of two pitches which are an octave apart it would look like this:

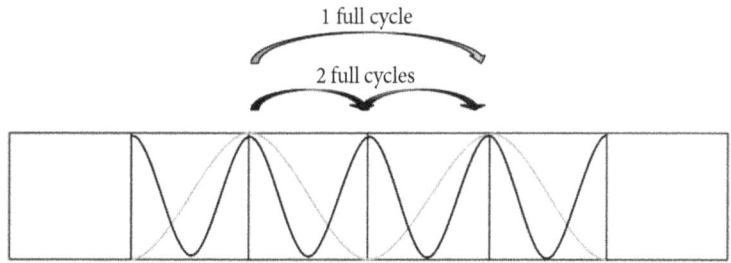

When you see this diagram, you should in fact imagine choirs of angels singing, and a blinding flash of light, and some of those special effects that happened when you reached the end of a platform game from the nineties. Because here's the magical thing: when we play two pitches that are exactly one octave apart, they actually sound like versions of *the same note*. What does this mean? This is hard to describe in words, but it's something we're all familiar with from music. One possible metaphor is to imagine climbing a circular staircase in a very tall tower: if we start at any position and keep walking upwards we'll soon get (in some sense) to "the same place again;" when we look out the window we'll see exactly the same views, just from slightly higher up.

Of course, the magic doesn't stop with just two waves. Remember when we added another *dashed* wave to our diagram, that had double the frequency of the black wave (and so four times the frequency of the grey wave)? It looked like this:

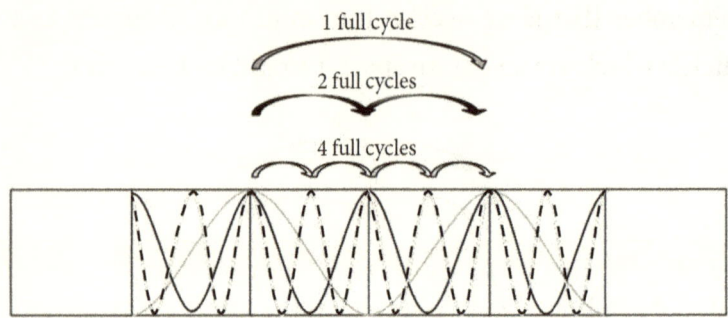

Since the dashed wave is double the frequency of the black wave, those two sound "the same" to us as well. And we already know that since the black wave is twice the frequency of the grey wave, *those* two sound "the same." And since the dashed wave and the grey wave both sound like the black wave, naturally the dashed wave sounds like the grey wave also. In this way, every wave sounds the same as any wave that is any whole number of octaves higher or lower than it.

Feeling Strangely Fine

Of course, like dollars and cents or feet and inches, for practical purposes we also need a smaller unit to measure intervals. In music, the standard "small" unit for measuring intervals is called a **semitone**, which we can define as "the interval between two notes such that twelve semitones make an octave."

It's important to understand that the difference in frequency between two notes a semitone apart is not equal to 1/12 of the difference in frequency between two notes an octave apart. The frequency difference that defines a semitone interval varies (in the same way that we saw the difference in frequency between octaves varied), but the relative difference in frequencies remains the same from one semitone to the next. For what it's worth, semitones are constructed such that each note has a frequency roughly 1.059 times higher than the one before it: if we started off with a pitch at 1000 Hz, then one semitone higher would be 1059 Hz, which is 1000 times 1.059, which is obviously very easy to calculate, and gives us a semitone whose absolute length is 59 Hz. But one semitone higher than 1059 Hz would be 1059 times 1.059, which comes out at 1122 Hz, and that gives us a semitone length of 63 Hz (the difference between 1122 Hz and 1059 Hz). The frequency difference that defines a semitone interval gets larger in absolute terms as we get higher and higher. It goes back to the coffee-cup example: the *absolute* difference (in ounces) between the cup-sizes got bigger and bigger as we moved towards the larger cups, but the *relative* difference between the cup sizes was completely constant.

Let's get back to our soundwave diagrams. If we start with a note that looks like this:

Then the soundwave one semitone higher will have an ever-so-slightly higher pitch; its peaks will be ever-so-slightly closer together, such that it completes a full cycle ever-so-slightly quicker:

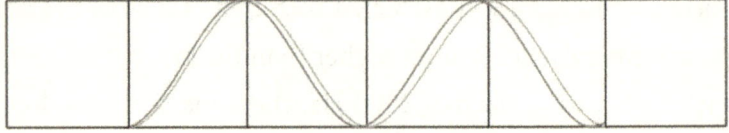

In terms of frequencies, that pair of soundwaves might look like this:

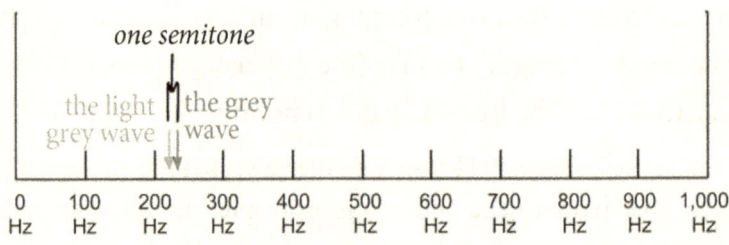

While it wouldn't come across very clearly if we drew many more waves on our diagram (we would just end up with a tangly mess), if we kept adding waves that were one semitone higher than each other then after twelve steps we would land at the black wave we saw earlier, one octave higher than the grey wave we started with:

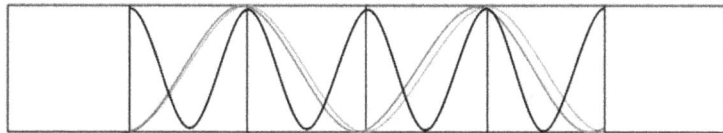

In terms of frequencies, we can see where each of those semitones would fall along the course of the octave. Each of the twelve semitone intervals sounds like "the same gap" to our ears although the frequency difference that defines a semitone is getting bigger and bigger:

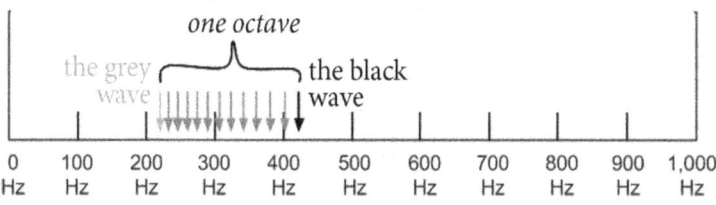

By this point, you may be wondering why we work with a system where there are twelve notes in an octave. The octave itself makes sense, because (as we said) two pitches an octave apart sound fundamentally "the same," so it makes sense that the octave is used as an interval. But why not split the octave into five notes, or seven notes, or any other number? Unfortunately, we're going to have to get a little hand-wavy here: some musical systems do use other numbers of notes, and the reasons that we ended up with specifically twelve notes in an octave in Western music are partly historical, partly mathematical, and entirely complicated. Still, we'll see later how our twelve-note system works to create some very harmonious music.

Given by the Mountains

By this point we're making very excellent progress. We already have a bunch of notes at different pitches, and a system of measurement to tell how far apart they are:

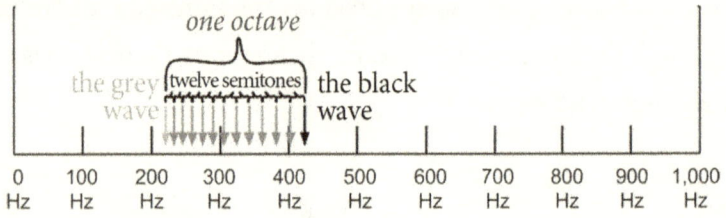

However, there's a very noticeable problem with the system we've used so far: we haven't given our notes any names. We can't say "hey Frankie, play *the grey wave*" because our choice of wave-colours has been completely arbitrary (and of course the wave isn't actually grey, or orange, or any other colour). This won't do at all. It's like having twelve kids and not naming any of them: how are you ever going to call them in from the yard?

By convention, musicians in the English-speaking world have developed names for each note so that they can talk about them among themselves. Seven of those notes have very easy names: they're named after the English letters *A-G*. For example, suppose the "grey wave" in our diagram is named *A*:

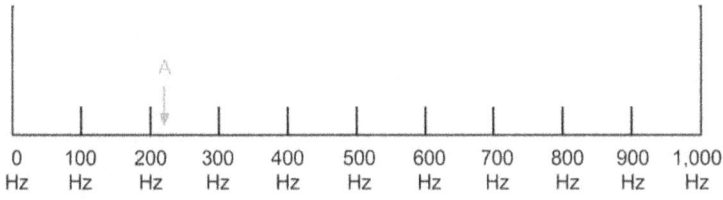

As we said, seven of our twelve notes are very conveniently named by the English letters *A-G*; we're going to "zoom in" a little from the previous diagram so we can see them more clearly:

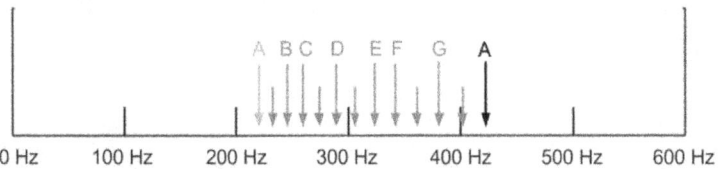

How about those notes in between them? That's a tiny bit more complicated: let's move over to the piano to find out.

It is not at all a coincidence that the pattern of white and black keys on a piano repeats in cycles of twelve. The keys follow a certain pattern every octave, and that pattern repeats up and down along the length of the keyboard:

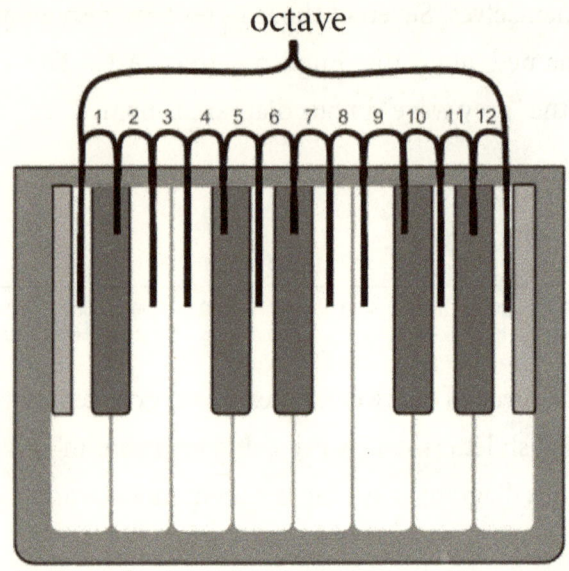

Repeated along the length of the piano, those octaves look like this:

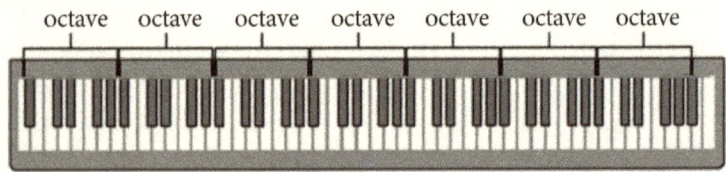

It is also not at all a coincidence that that pattern of twelve keys is composed of seven white keys and five black keys. These are the seven notes named after the letters *A-G*:

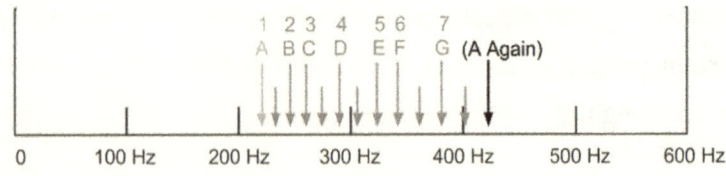

And they are *exactly* the same as the seven white keys on the piano:

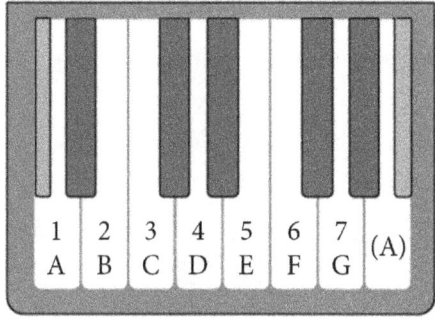

How about those pesky black keys, though? You're right, they need names, too. These keys are named relative to the white keys on either side of them. Take this particular black key, for instance:

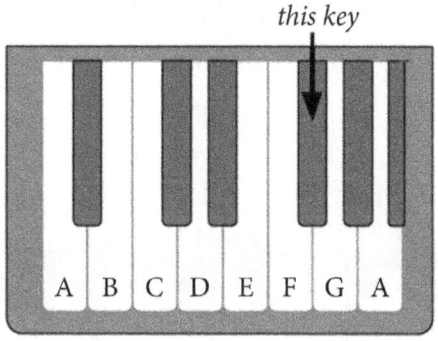

This black key is one semitone above *F*, and one semitone below *G*. We have a special symbol that denotes "one semitone above": it looks like this: (♯). We call this symbol **sharp**, and we can call the note **F-sharp**, written "$F^\sharp$." We also have a special symbol that denotes "one semitone below," it looks like this (♭), and we call it **flat**.

So we can also call this same note **G-flat**, written G♭:

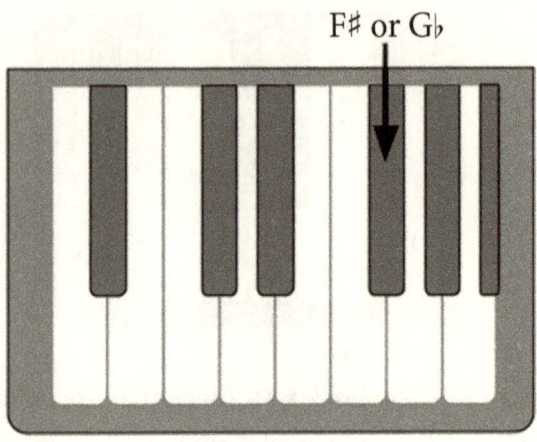

All of the black keys have two common names, one determined by the white key immediately before it and one determined by the white key immediately after it, as follows:

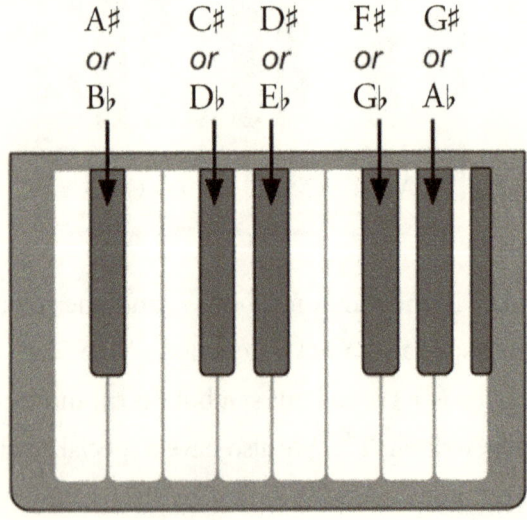

How does a musician know which of these names to use on any particular occasion? Essentially, note-naming follows a rule we could call "minimise confusion." For example, suppose we're playing a tune that includes the notes G and E, as well as a note that could be referred to as either *F-sharp* or *G-flat*. In this case, we'll call the note *F-sharp* and the written-out tune might look something like this:

G — F-sharp — F-sharp — E — E — F-sharp — G

Why? Because this prevents any of the confusion we would have if we named the note *G-flat* in this context, where we're also using a G. As an analogy: imagine that there are two common versions of your name: Jan and Janice. If you're hanging around in a group which has someone whose name sounds a lot like Jan you will probably go by Janice, but if you're hanging around in a group someone else whose name sounds like Janice then you'll probably go by Jan.

Filling Out The Octave

We're nearly finished, now, with everything we need to know about how notes are named — we just need to put together a few of the ideas we've seen so far. In the last section we figured out how to name all the notes in a little stretch of the spectrum:

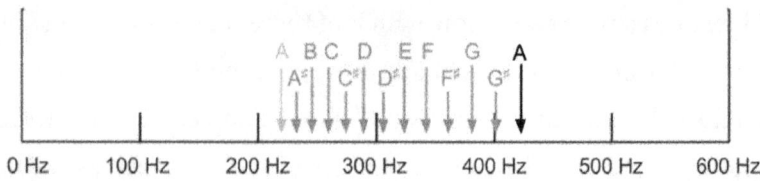

(Each of those smaller arrows of course has two names, but things are already pretty squished on the diagram so we're only mentioning one of them).

Now: we already know that when we double the frequency of any note we get the same note an octave higher, and we already have one example of this in our diagram with a lower and higher *A*. However, we could also double the higher *A* (at 440 Hz) to get an even higher *A* at 880 Hz:

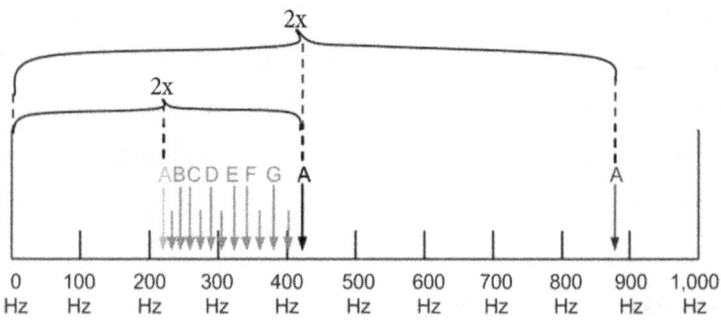

If we double the frequency of any of the other notes, we'll also get another version of that same note. Suppose we focus for the moment on just *A* and *B*. Our first *B* is two semitones above our lowest *A*, which was at 220 Hz. Since the frequency of every note is approximately 1.059 times higher than the note a semitone below it, going from *A* to *B* means multiplying 220 Hz by (approximately) 1.059 and then multiplying the outcome by 1.059 again. This means that *B* is roughly 1.059 × 1.059 × the frequency of *A*, which comes out to 1.121 × the frequency of *A*. Therefore, our first *B* is 1.121 × 220 Hz, which is approximately 247 Hz:

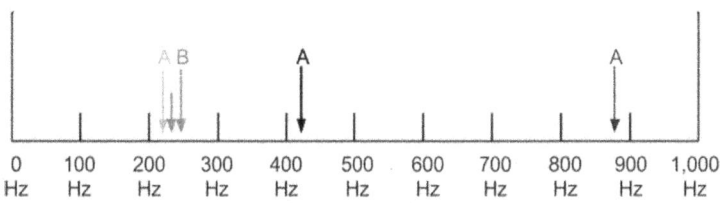

What if we want to find another *B*? As you'd expect, we can double the frequency of our first *B* (at 247 Hz) to get our new *B*, and doubling 247 Hz gives us 494 Hz:

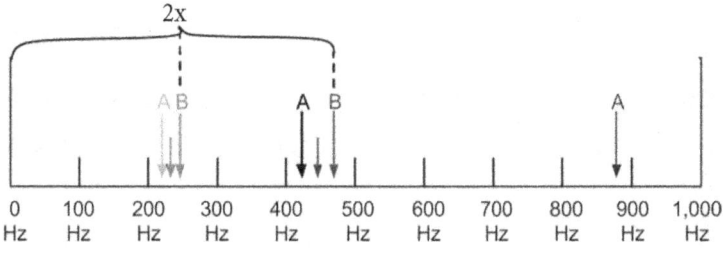

You'll notice that this new *B* is also two semitones above our second *A*, so its frequency should be 1.121 times higher than that *A*. Is it? Well, that A is at 440 Hz, and if we multiply 440 Hz by 1.121 we do indeed get (approximately) 494 Hz! This is a wonderful property of the kind of mathematical pattern that we're looking at here, where every term in a sequence is determined by a ratio to the one before: everything stays perfectly in proportion as we move up the scale!

Finally, we can add one more *B* on our diagram at double the frequency of our second *B*. 494 Hz multiplied by 2 is 988 Hz:

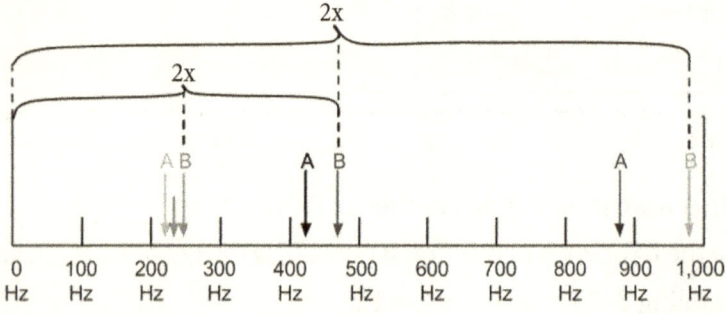

To check our work, we can take the pitch of the highest *A* (which is 880 Hz) and multiply it by 1.121 to see if it equals the frequency of the highest *B* — again, we get (approximately) 988 Hz, as we should!

Of course, there's nothing at all stopping us there — we could keep climbing up the spectrum and find higher and higher *A*'s and *B*'s by doubling pitches. And (of course) there's nothing at all special about *A* or *B* either: if we keep doubling the pitches of all our notes, we get many repetitions of full and complete octaves:

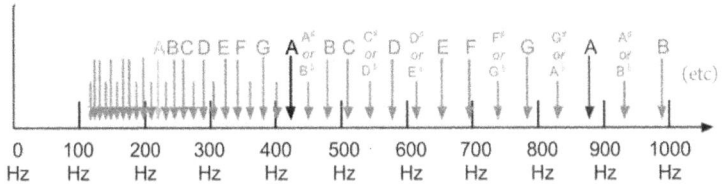

If you had a long enough piano you could keep going a very long way in both directions. But we all have to live with the piano we have, not the piano we wish we had.

Standard Always

So far in this book, we've repeatedly built our story around an *A* note at 440 Hz; at first we just told you to "suppose" there was a soundwave whose pitch was 440 Hz, and later to "suppose" that this was a note named *A*:

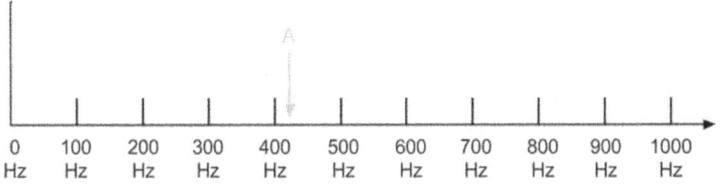

But there's clearly a continuous spectrum of pitches, and it's not yet clear why 440 Hz became the lucky owner of a note of its own, while 430 Hz and 450 Hz are the kids who never got picked for the basketball team. Let's look at our old favourite metaphor to explore the situation here; let's return again to Yaff's Caff, where the size of each coffee-cup is determined relative to the size of the cup before it. In our example from earlier, each cup was ⅓ bigger than the previous cup:

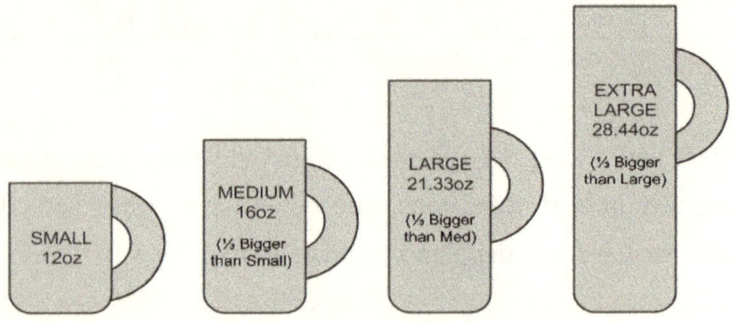

This is all well and good, but… as with our question about what pitch our *A* would be at, how did we decide what size a "Small" would be? Our current answer, "12 oz," is completely arbitrary: we could have made a Small be 10 oz, or 13 oz, or (for that matter) 11.051981 oz or anything else at all. If we started with a "Small" at 10 oz, for example, but kept the "⅓ bigger each time" rule, then we'd end up with this set of cups:

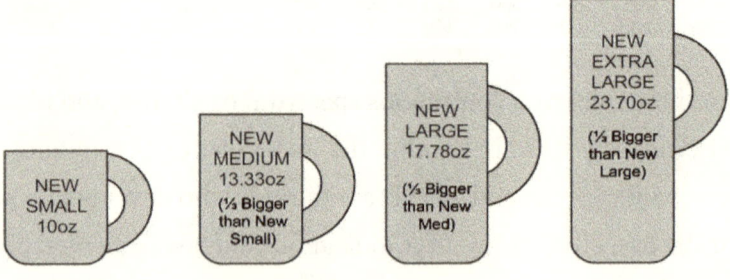

Similarly, the spectrum of possible soundwaves is continuous: we could (in theory) place *A* at 430 Hz, or 450 Hz, or anywhere else as well:

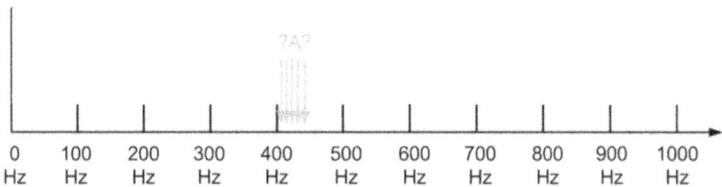

And the decision of where to put our *A* has knock-on consequences for all the other notes, because the rules of octaves and semitones determine where the notes above and below it have to go. We can't simply pick up and move all the notes a fixed (linear) distance; the notes will move in relative proportion according to where we put our *A*.

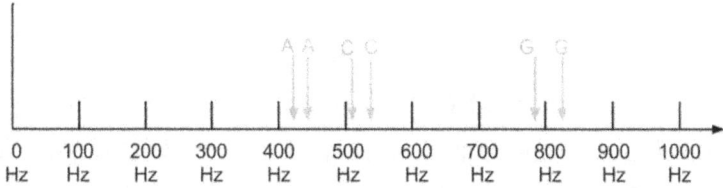

It turns out that, because of the way that music works, any of these choices of *A* would be just fine. Since the rest of the notes would all keep their relative distances from each other, and our ears perceive music according to relative frequencies, we could in fact put *A* at any of these places and come out with beautiful music. What really matters is that musicians playing together are using one consistent standard — that everyone's *A* is in the same place. If a band tuned all its instruments correctly against the lead guitar then it wouldn't even matter if none of them knew exactly what pitch they were playing — the music would still work out beautifully. As such, historically, this particular *A* has ranged from about 415 Hz to about 465 Hz.

While 415-465 might sound like a pretty big range, a good analogy might be to imagine a couple of remote villages a few hundred years ago where everyone in each village timed their own pocket-watch to the local church clock. It mattered that everyone within each village kept the same time, but did it really matter if the church clocks themselves were not in time with each other, even by quite a large margin?

However, as the world becomes more interconnected, it has become more important that all of us are standardising on the same clocks — and that all musicians are standardising on the same pitches. Nowadays, this particular *A* generally lives at 440 Hz:

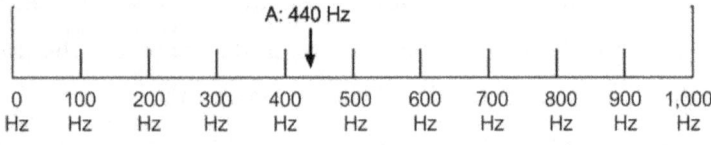

And isn't it nice to know that it has a safe, permanent home?

This *A* at 440 Hz, which is called **Concert A**, is the standard used for tuning instruments. For example, if you go to see an orchestra, Concert *A* is the note that all the orchestra members will play together before they start a performance (often as soon as they all get on stage), to make sure their instruments are properly tuned to each other. Concert *A* is easy to find on a piano:

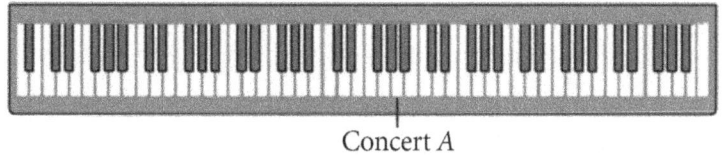

Concert *A*

And the same note corresponds to the "*A*-string" on a violin:

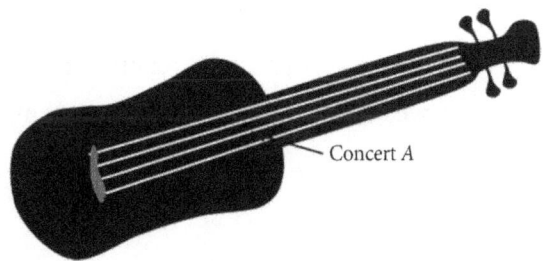

And also to this combination of fingers on a flute:

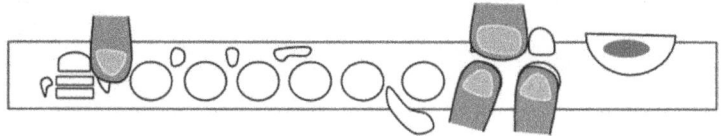

And so on, for (almost all) the other instruments in the orchestra. Some instruments, such as the tuba and the piccolo, can't play Concert *A* because it's out of the range of notes that can be played on the instrument. But these instruments can play an *A* in another octave and try as best they can to make it sound like it's a perfect octave or two away from Concert *A* as they tune. It's a tough job, being Concert *A*, there's a lot of pressure on your wave-like shoulders, but 440 Hz does the job with distinction.

La Donna è Mobile

One really fascinating outcome of the fact that our brains perceive music through the relative frequencies of notes is that we can actually "pick up and move" a tune to a different start-point and it will still feel recognisable (though, of course, not exactly identical). How does this work? It's simply a result of the fact that sound is perceived according to relative frequencies. For example: suppose we start a tune with the note *A*, and follow it up with the note *D*:

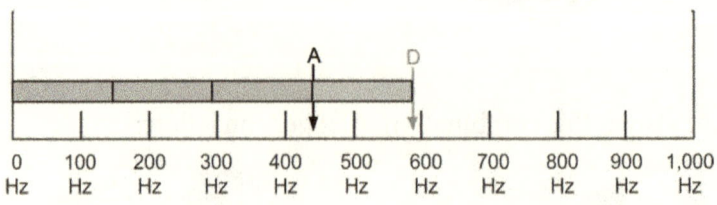

It happens that the frequency of *D* is almost-exactly ⅓ higher than the frequency of *A*, so we are moving from one note (*A*) to the note that has a frequency ⅓ higher than it (*D*). Suppose, though, that we'd prefer to start on a different note — for example, that we want to start on that same *D*. What should our "next note" be so that the pattern will sound similar to our ears? Well, clearly we should move from *D* to the note that has a frequency ⅓ higher than it. That turns out to be *G*:

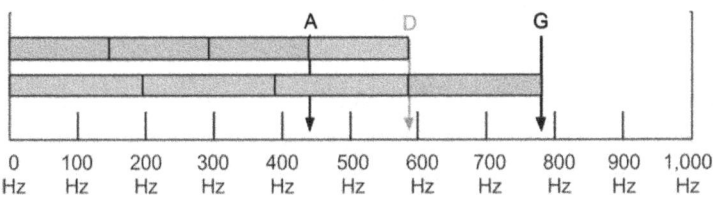

If we look at *A*, *D* and *G* on our piano and measure the intervals between those notes, we'll find something interesting that (once again) is not at all a coincidence:

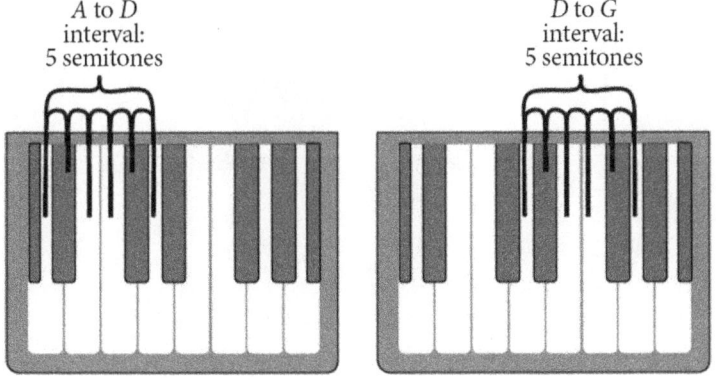

The interval between *A* and *D* is five semitones, and the interval between *D* and *G* is also five semitones! Because all notes are designed to be the same relative distance from each other, we can get the "equivalent" version of a tune which starts on a different note simply by adding or subtracting a fixed number of semitones from every note in the tune. This, of course, is an incredibly useful feature of our musical system, and it didn't just happen by accident — it's a specific consequence of how neatly organised the musical system is.

How does this work with an actual song? Imagine your friend Mike starts singing the well-known spiritual *Amazing Grace*; he might begin on a comfortable *A*:

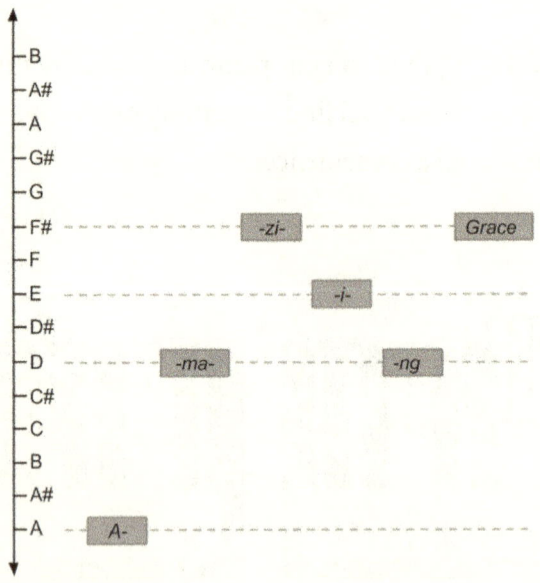

However, your friend Deborah might have a higher-pitched voice, and might like singing a little higher up. That's not a problem: she can simply "pick up and move" the tune to some higher notes. Perhaps she could start the tune on *D*, instead:

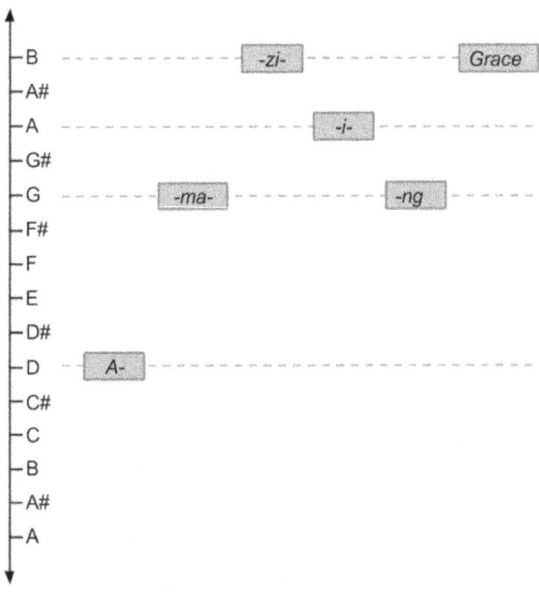

Now, if Mike and Deborah are trying to sing the song together, they'll have to agree on a start-note. But if we listened to Mike sing his starting-on-*A* version one day, and listened to Deborah sing her starting-on-*D* version the next day, we would say to ourselves "hey! that sounds like the same song!" So long as they're following the same pattern — adding or subtracting the same number of semitones from every note in the song — it doesn't matter which note they start on:

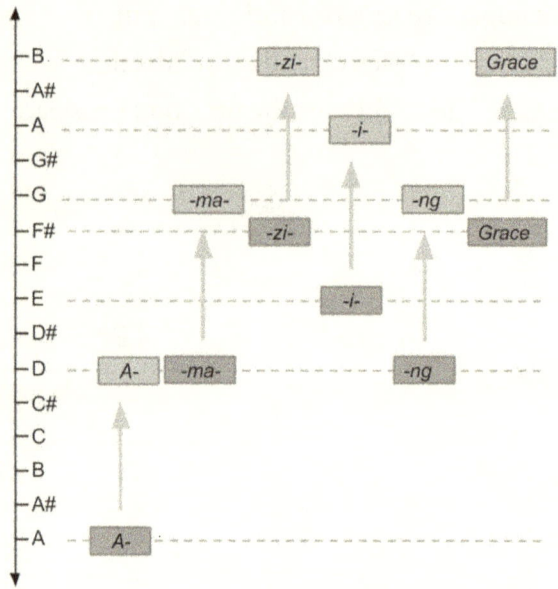

We see this very clearly in the case of *Somewhere Over the Rainbow*: both Frank Sinatra and Judy Garland sing fabulous renditions of this song, and while Frank Sinatra's starts on a low *D*-flat and Judy Garland's starts on a higher *A*-flat, we recognize the same tune in both cases!

Well — it's been quite a ride. In this chapter alone we've discovered pitches, invented note-names, and figured out how they're all related to each other. But we can't just pick any of the notes we know and create a tune; there are specific patterns underlying the notes we use in each song, as we'll see in the next chapter.

Scales

The sound of an orchestra differs from the sound of a car crash in that orchestral sounds contain very *distinct* pitches. A car driving into a lampost will exude all kinds of vibrations at all kinds of different frequencies, but a musical instrument is specifically designed to enable us to create sounds that are dominated by one specific frequency at any given time. Yet, the sound of an orchestra is still a conglomeration of many different notes, coming from many different instruments. Why do orchestras sound like a chorus of angels, rather than a chorus of cats?

In order for orchestras to sound like music to our ears, composers very carefully choose a distinct set of notes to use in any given song that will make sure the notes that are played fit very well together. The set of notes they choose to use in a given piece of music is called a **scale**. Technically, a scale is just any collection of musical notes organised according to their frequency (from lowest to highest, or highest to lowest). However, there are fascinating rules behind which notes go into all the commonly-used scales that are actually used in the music we commonly listen to — rules that we'll learn all about very shortly.

The Colours of the Scale

To understand scales, let's first look at a metaphor.

Imagine you're thinking of re-painting your house. You go to a paint store and find that they have twelve different colours of paint available, but they offer them to customers in sets of seven. This is because there are certain sets of colours that work very well together — sets that "look right" when used in combination with each other. If you were to use one set of these colours and then suddenly add in some different colour (one of the ones outside the set), it would just viscerally *look wrong*. It's not that you'd be violating some intellectual or theoretical rules about which colours *should* look good together: it's that you would quite instinctively look at the new combination and feel discombobulated by it.

The sets of paints, of course, are a metaphor for scales. In Western music, we use twelve different notes in music as a whole but we always use them in certain scales — in certain "sets." And, like in our metaphor, it's usually very easy to hear if someone is playing you a tune and accidentally hits a note that doesn't belong in the scale they're playing in. It feels wrong, viscerally and instinctively. You don't need to be taught this — you'll just feel a little shiver up your spine.

To continue the metaphor, notice that the store *isn't* telling you what shapes or patterns to paint on your walls — once you've taken the set of colours home, you can paint them in any order or any combinations, some of which will certainly look better than others (which depends on your tastes and talents as a painter). And you don't need to use all seven colours in any particular room, if you don't want to. But what the store is saying is *"these colours are guaranteed to go well together — if you choose the colours from among one of the pre-arranged sets we provide you with, we can guarantee that none of them will look 'jarring' together."*

Similarly, a musician can pick any combination of notes from within a given scale and combine them in many different and interesting ways in order to create a tune. And some of these tunes will sound better than others, and of course people have different tastes in music the same way people have different tastes in the nicest ways to arrange colours on the walls of a room. Again, though, so long as a musician has picked notes from within a single scale, the result won't sound jarring — even if it doesn't necessarily inspire.

This is made ever-so-slightly more complicated by that fact that, if you're a really good painter with an excellent eye for design, maybe you'll occasionally want to throw in a colour that *doesn't* belong in the set you're painting with. Very occasionally, and with great care, and only a splash, you could add a colour from outside the set — it will certainly draw the viewer's eye. In a sense it will still seem "jarring," but if you're talented at throwing in the jarring notes then they can be jarring in a "good" way — or at least, "good" for some of your viewers' tastes!

For the less-talented painters among us, though, it is probably good to stick with paints from a single set. And, similarly, if you want to stay "safe" you should be playing notes from a single scale. In fact, almost-all music we hear is almost-always working from within a single scale, so there's no shame or beginner-ness in sticking within a scale.

In fact, incidentally, some instruments such as the harmonica are designed to *only* play notes within a single scale. This is why it is relatively difficult to make an unpleasant sound on a good-quality harmonica (though it is *very* possible to make unpleasant sounds on a cheap, plasticky harmonica). Since the notes are in a single scale, you can play them in any order at all and they'll sound like they "fit" — whether or not you can play any recognisable tunes. This is not true, for example, on a piano — you can easily play a combination of notes on the piano that will cause the listener to reflexively "jerk," because it just sounds *wrong*.

Let's go back to the paint store to highlight something interesting going on here. There are only twelve colours at the store, and there are many different sets of paints, most of which contain seven colours each. As such, many different sets have a lot of overlap between them. This means that the same colours that go well together in one set suddenly become jarring when they're seen alongside certain other colours. For example, perhaps a certain shade of blue doesn't look jarring when placed with yellow and orange, but blue suddenly *does* look jarring when placed with yellow and red (just hypothetically — please don't take design tips from a book about music!).

Similarly, with music, the feeling of "jarringness" we get from out-of-scale notes is all to do with the other notes we've just heard. Any two notes will be featured together in *some* commonly-heard scale or other, but once you add a third note.... you may be moving outside the scale, and the combination could suddenly sound "wrong."

Finally, it's important to be aware that there are sets of paints with different "moods." Some sets of colours give an overall "happy" feel when used together; other sets feel "sad" together (in a non-jarring way). Again, this isn't just an academic distinction or something decided by experts — this is something that you just "feel" when you see things painted with the different sets of colours. Certain sets just inspire happy feelings in the viewers, and certain sets just (somehow) feel sad. Similarly, then, the two most common types of scales in Western music are **Major Scales** and **Minor Scales**, where Major Scales generally sound happy and positive to us, while Minor Scales generally sound sad and melancholy.

Now — exactly how accurate is the metaphor of the paint store for music? What are its limitations? There are two main dis-similarities to be aware of. First, if such a paint-store existed, its combinations would probably be much more opinion-based than scales in music are. There are definitely certain colours that go well together, and certain colours that seem jarring when used together, but our feelings about colour are just not as deep-rooted or as visceral as our feelings about music.

Second, and relatedly, the way scales work is beautiful and mathematically consistent in a way that colour-sets probably wouldn't be. As we've already talked about in the "pitch" chapter, all musical notes are just slightly stretched or squeezed versions of "the same thing" — they're all just sound-waves with different wavelengths. As a result, there is a really beautiful logic and symmetry to how scales are constructed…. which we'll talk about next.

A First Great Scale
Let's start by looking at a very common scale that starts on *C*: it's

called C Major, and it's found in all kinds of popular music. If you remember from our paint-store metaphor, a scale is just a set of notes that go well together — if we make up a tune and only use notes from within that set then we can guarantee that every note will "get along well" with the others, and that none of them will sound jarring. The seven notes in the C Major Scale are as follows:

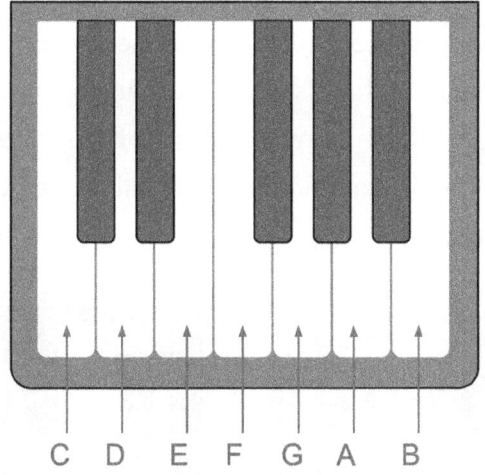

Suppose, now, that we wanted to make another "Major" Scale that starts on the note "B":

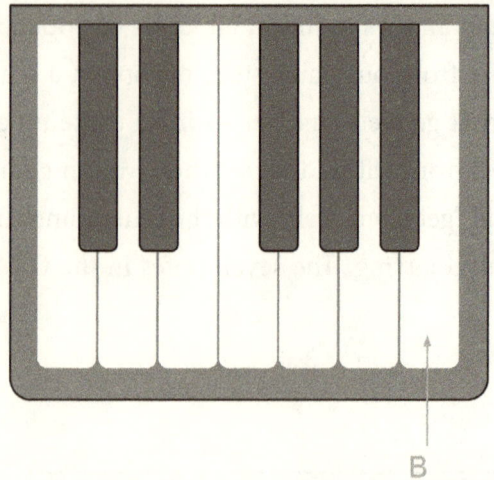

The fact that it is also a Major Scale means that is somehow "sounds" similar — that it's a somehow analogous set of notes, just starting at a different place on the piano. It turns out that the notes in the B-Major Scale are the following ones, with the following names:

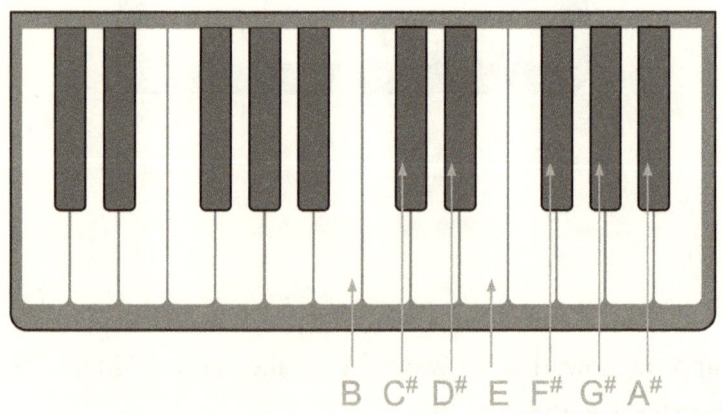

Now, this doesn't look anywhere near as pretty and convenient as the C Major Scale. Many of the notes here are black keys, and the black keys have funny names.

However, if you're almost inhumanly sharp-eyed, you might notice a pattern here. Let's look at the number of "hops" we take to reach each of the keys in each of the scales — we'll start with C Major. While the black keys are smaller on the piano and may seem like they're "less involved" somehow, the interval between any two neighbouring keys on a piano (musically speaking) is exactly the same whether they're black or white: any two neighbouring piano-keys are *always* exactly a semitone apart. (If two white keys have a black key between them, then there's one semitone between the first white key and the black key, another semitone between the black key and the next white key, and *two* semitones between the white keys.)

C MAJOR SCALE:

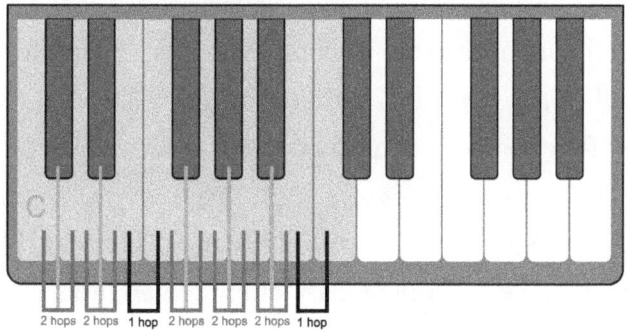

PATTERN: 2 hop - 2 hop - **1 hop** - 2 hop - 2 hop - 2 hop - **1 hop**

The B Major Scale, it turns out, follows *exactly* the same pattern: we've just shifted the hop-pattern further along the piano so that it starts on a *B*:

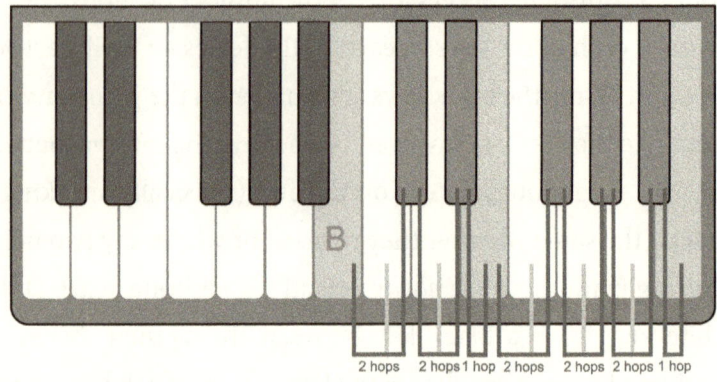

PATTERN: 2 hop - 2 hop - 1 hop - 2 hop - 2 hop - 2 hop - 1 hop

In fact, it turns out that *all* Major Scales follow exactly the same pattern of hops — the only difference between them is the note that they start on. As such, musicians have developed a special "general" language to talk about these scales, so that we can discuss all of them together rather than going through the same details for every particular case.

The Very Model of a Modern Major, Generally

Imagine you're teaching a class of kindergarteners how to do prints with potatoes (if you've never tried this, it's a lot of fun.

The printing, that is, though the teaching could be fun too). Each of the kids has been given a potato-half with some kind of shape engraved in it: some of the kids have a duck-shape, some have a cat, some have a weird oblong shape because you screwed up your duck-engraving but you tell the kid it's actually a cloud. Anyway: you stand in front of the class and give them instructions on what to do next: "take your potato-half; dip it in the ink; shake off any excess ink; put your potato on the page; press down; lift it up; you have a print!"

These instructions use a general form for all the kids ("take your potato-half, *regardless of what's engraved in it*; dip it in the ink..."), and it would clearly be a waste of time to use specific forms of address for every child individually: "if you have a duck-print: take that duck, dip it in the ink...." and then "if you have a cat-print: take that cat, dip it in the ink..." and so on indefinitely. The relevant part of the procedure is the same regardless of what shape the kid is starting with, so it makes sense to talk about it in general rather than repeating yourself by covering every possible specific iteration.

Similarly, musicians have a special language for talking about the general case of a major scale, that saves a lot of time and effort and highlights the fact that the underlying pattern is the same in all cases. You may actually be familiar with this special language because Fraulein Maria sang it to us in that famous movie/musical *The Sound of Music*. You might recall the scene where Maria sits in a field with a guitar, surrounded by the Von Trapp children, and launches into a song about the "ABC's" of music:

Do (a deer, a female deer)
Re (a drop of golden sun)
Mi (a name, I call myself)
Fa (a long, long way to run)
So (a needle pulling thread)
La (a note to follow So)
Ti (a drink with jam and bread)
...that will bring us back to Do (Do Do Do...)!

This language of "*Do Re Mi*" can be used to describe any Major Scale whatsoever. Depending on which specific scale we're interested in, *Do* might represent *C*, or it might represent *B*, or it might represent *any* of the other notes in Western music.[1] But whichever *Do* we're talking about, we'll be able to find the appropriate *Re* by jumping two semitones higher. Overall, the pat-

---

[1] There are two systems for using *Do, Re, Mi, Fa, So, La,* and *Ti* to refer to musical notes. In the "movable Do" system, highlighted here, *Do* always refers to the first note of a Major Scale, regardless of what the pitch of that note is. There is an alternative system called "fixed Do" in which *Do, Re, Mi, Fa, So, La,* and *Ti* are simply alternative names for the notes C, D, E, F, G, A, and B, which is used widely outside the English-speaking world.

tern of intervals for *Do Re Mi* will always look like this:

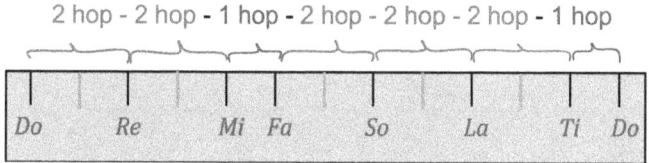

And every particular Major Scale is just a concrete iteration of that same pattern. So, for example, in the B Major scale the *Do* maps onto *B* and the rest of the mapping looks like this:

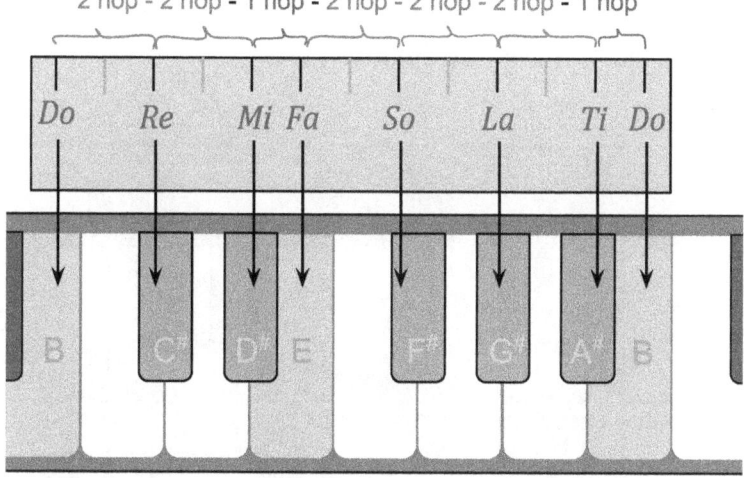

Whereas in the C Major scale the *Do* maps onto *C* and the rest of the mapping looks like this:

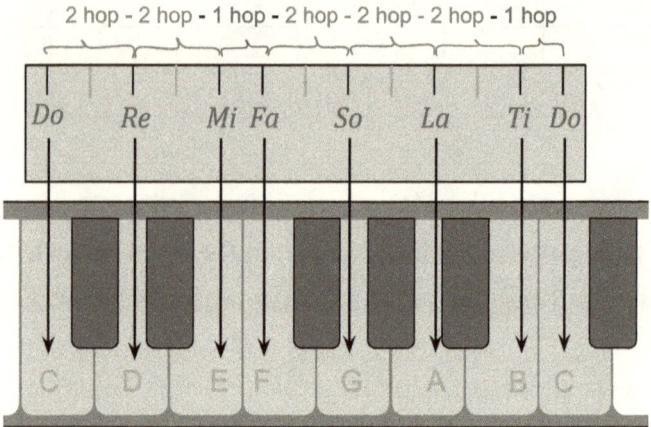

C MAJOR SCALE:

But the two scales line up perfectly; they are exactly the same pattern, just starting on a different note:

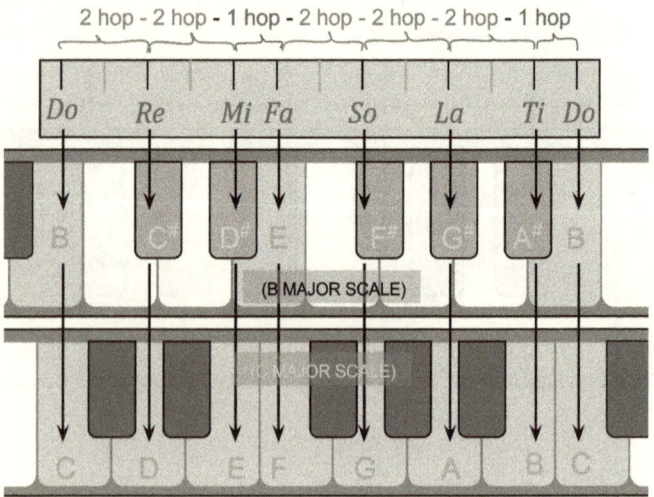

Now, we already know that the pattern on a piano repeats many times; as such, once we get back to *Do*, we can start all over again there. The only limit is the size of our piano; in theory, we could keep repeating these *Do Re Mi* patterns forever:

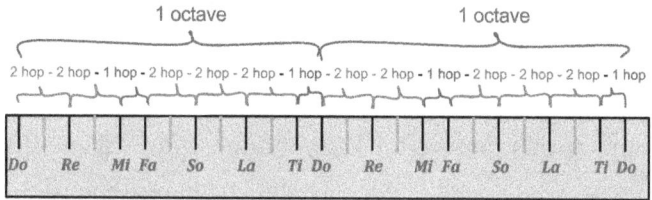

Lived a Minor

While Fraulein Maria introduces us only to the Major Scale, you won't be surprised to hear that other types of scales tend to follow a similar "blueprint": they are essentially a pattern of hops, which can be started off at different notes to give us different scales. Alongside the Major Scale, the other common type of scale (and these two are far and away the most commonly-found scales in Western music) is the Minor Scale. The generalised names we give to the notes of the Minor Scale have never been immortalised in popular song but one common way to name them is *Do - Re - Me - Fa - So - Le - Te - Do*. You may have noticed that the names look very similar to the names in the Major Scale; except that the Minor Scale uses "Me," "Le," and "Te" instead of the "Mi," "La" and "Ti" used in the Major Scale. These slightly different names indicate that each of these notes is one semitone lower in the Minor Scale than its Major Scale equivalent. So, the pattern of hops for a Minor Scale looks like this:

MINOR SCALE PATTERN:
2 hop - 1 hop - 2 hop - 2 hop - 1 hop - 2 hop - 2 hop

Do   Re   Me   Fa   So   Le   Te   Do

If you stare at this picture for long enough, you will eventually begin to feel sad. However, that may just be because you wasted an entire afternoon staring at a picture of a hop-pattern. Amazingly, while the Major Scale and Minor Scale patterns are just very-slightly-different sequences of hops, the effect that these different patterns have on us musically is profound. The Major Scale is used to compose most happy music — think of the Christmas hymn *Joy to the World*, the Beatles belting out *I Want to Hold Your Hand*, or Michel Telo singing *Ai Se Eu Te Pego*. Meanwhile, the Minor Scale is used for most sad music — think Beethoven's *Fur Elise*, the folk song *House of the Rising Sun*, or basically any of the heartbreaking music from Antony and the Johnsons.

As before, every specific iteration of the minor scale is just this same pattern starting on a different note. So for example, the B Minor and C Minor scales looks like this:

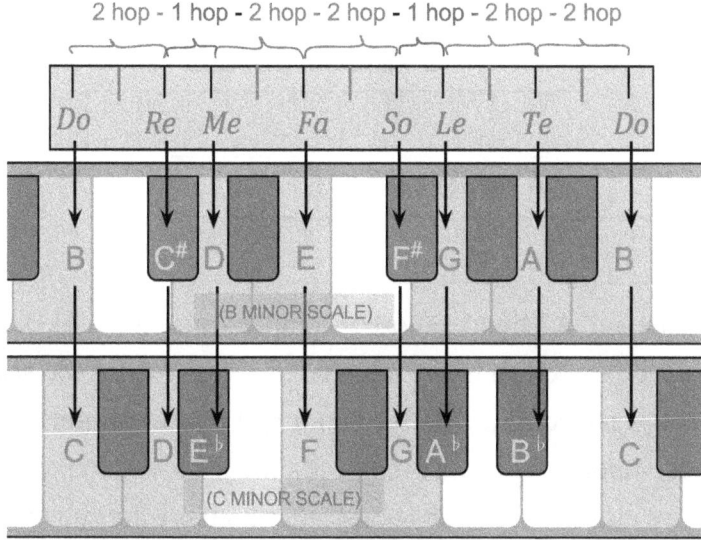

Jekyll and Hyde

We said at the beginning of the chapter that a scale is like a color palette - the particular set of notes we use to create our musical masterpiece.

In fact, just as we can create paintings with a variety of different moods using the same set of paints, it is possible for the same set of scale-notes to take on different personalities. The same set of notes can even be used in both a Major and a Minor Scale - in one case they'll sound happy, in the other sad!

For example, let's take a look at the C Major and A Minor Scales below. They both use the same set of notes - A, B, C, D, E, F, and G!

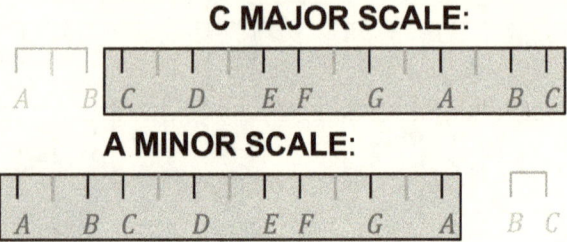

C Major and A Minor are sort of complements - a Dr. Jekyll and Mr. Hyde embodied in the same set of notes. We call two scales with this relationship **relative major** and **relative minor** scales, i.e., A Minor is the relative minor of C Major, and C Major is the relative major of A Minor, because they both use the same notes.

But if the same set of notes can become both a Major Scale or a Minor Scale, what makes pieces constructed using this set of notes sound happy in one case, and sad in the other? This has to do with how the notes are used in a particular piece of music.

To understand why, let's turn back to our painting analogy. If I've chosen my set of seven paints from the 12 available in the store - let's say each is a particular hue of red, orange, yellow, green, blue, indigo, and violet - there are a variety of ways I could use them when I paint my masterpiece. I could create a painting of the sea, where my most-used color is the blue. I could create a still life of a vase of roses, where the predominant color used is red.

Similarly, the starting note of the scale - which we call the **tonic** - is the focus of our particular piece of music. In a piece composed in C Major, the note C is often the starting point and destination of the melody, and is often where the resting points in between land. In a piece composed in A Minor, the note A is the focal point of the piece, and since the notes of the scale have a different relationship to A than they do to C - remember, a minor scale has a hop pattern of 2-1-2-2-1-2-2 instead of 2-2-1-2-2-2-1 - the mood of the piece ends up sounding quite different.

It is worth noting here another term we use to indicate the tonic note and scale used in a particular piece of music: its **key**. If a piece of music is composed using the C Major Scale, we can alternately say that the piece is "in the key of C Major," or if it uses the A Minor Scale, we can say it is "in the key of A Minor."

Relative Major and Minor

There is a relative Minor to every Major Scale, and vice versa. To see why, let's take a closer look at our Major and Minor hop patterns. A Major Scale has the following hop pattern: 2-2-1-2-2-2-1.

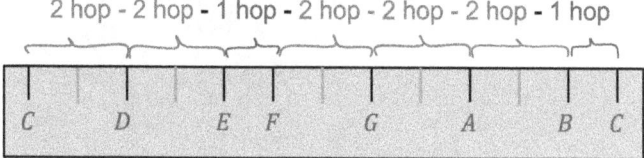

MAJOR SCALE PATTERN:
2 hop - 2 hop - 1 hop - 2 hop - 2 hop - 2 hop - 1 hop

And a Minor Scale has the following hop pattern: 2-1-2-2-1-2-2.

MINOR SCALE PATTERN:
2 hop - 1 hop - 2 hop - 2 hop - 1 hop - 2 hop - 2 hop

| A | B C | D | E F | G | A |

If we take the notes of our Major Scale, and simply designate A as the starting note instead of C, we get the A Minor Scale (we've drawn the notes in a circular pattern for easier visualisation):

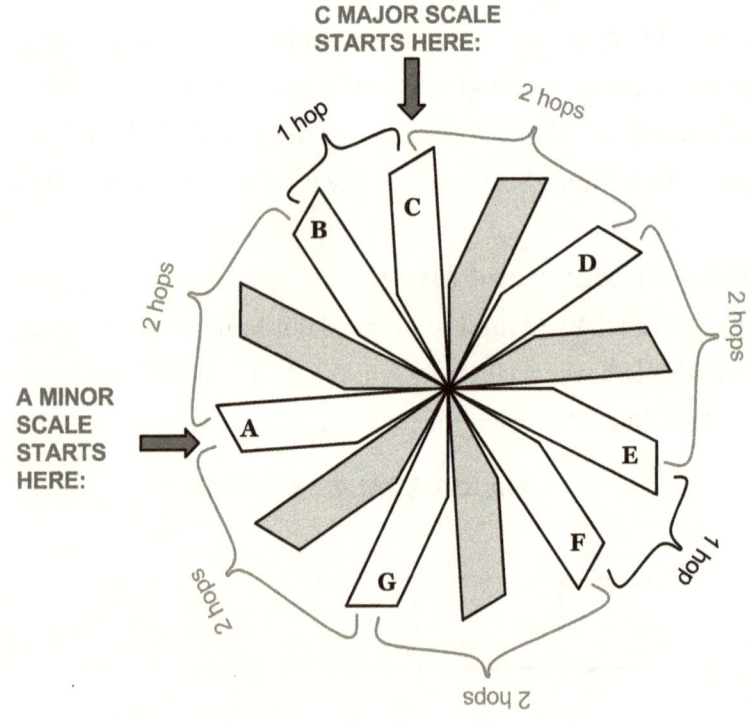

This is because the Minor Scale hop pattern is secretly the same as the Major Scale hop pattern, just starting at the sixth note in the Major Scale sequence! Similarly, if we take any Major Scale and start it off at the sixth note instead of the first note, we'll get a Minor Scale. Take a look at the G Major and E Minor Scales, for example:

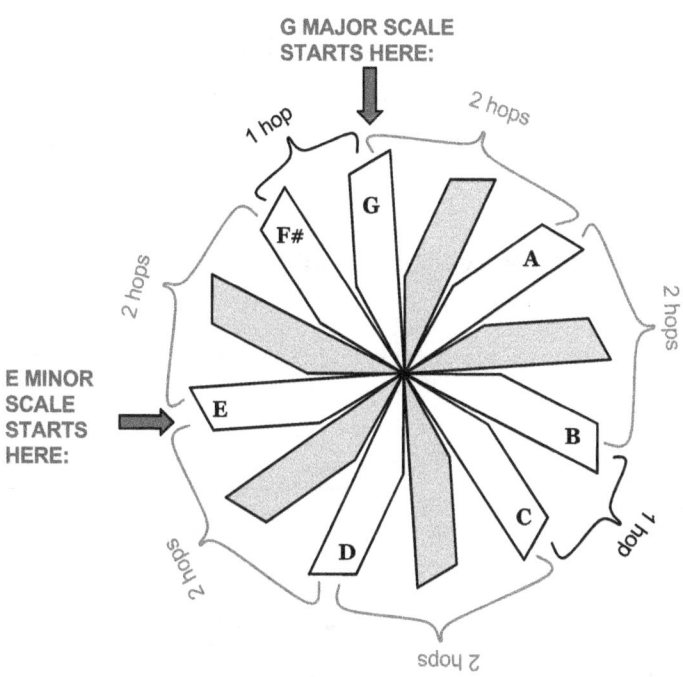

Since both of these scales use the same set of notes, E Minor is the relative minor of G Major, and G Major is the relative major of E Minor. Similarly, by constructing a scale starting on the sixth note of any Major Scale, we find its relative Minor.

Scaling Up

Even if the Major and Minor scales are the major players in the Western music scene,[2] even apart from sequential variations on this special hop pattern, there are other scales out there, each proudly doing its own thing. For example, there is a family of scales called **Pentatonic Scales** which have just five notes (instead of the seven notes in Major and Minor Scales). Here's an example of a Pentatonic Scale pattern often used in Chinese music:

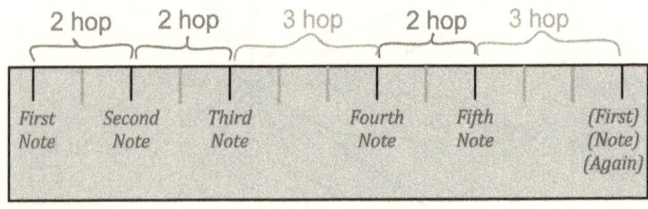

In Indian Carnatic music, scales can have a variety of numbers of notes; here's one basic, seven-note pattern:[3]

---

2 Slight modifications to the standard minor scale we introduced here also pop up frequently.
3 The intervals between notes of the Carnatic scale shown here using Western semitones are an approximation of the actual intervals used in Carnatic music.

A COMMON CARNATIC SCALE PATTERN:

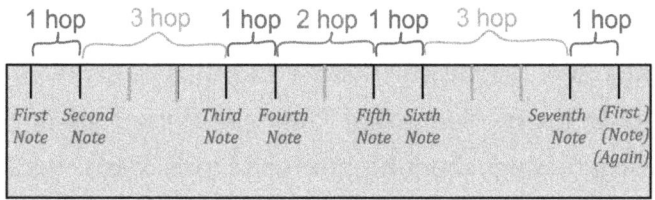

Meanwhile, one six-note scale used in blues music looks like this:

SIX-NOTE BLUES SCALE PATTERN:

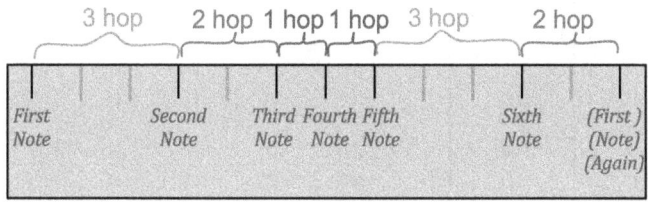

Even though scales can have different numbers of pitches, all scale-patterns across the world tend to span the distance covered by twelve semitones in total. The octave, that magical musical distance, seems to be quite fundamental across times and cultures, so it's the particular scale patterns (among other things) that sometimes makes music from different cultures sound immediately "different."

As you might by now expect, composers will sometimes deviate from common scale patterns to make their music sound more funky. Sometimes, they'll tactfully — at just the right moment — throw notes into a song that don't actually belong to the scale that the rest of the music is composed with, just to grab our attention. In the movie/musical *West Side Story,* Tony does just that when he sings about his newfound love, Maria. Recall the first line of the song: *'Maria,' I just met a girl named 'Maria'!* Though most of the song is composed in a major scale, the second note of "Maria" in the opening lyrics falls between the fourth and fifth notes of the major scale:

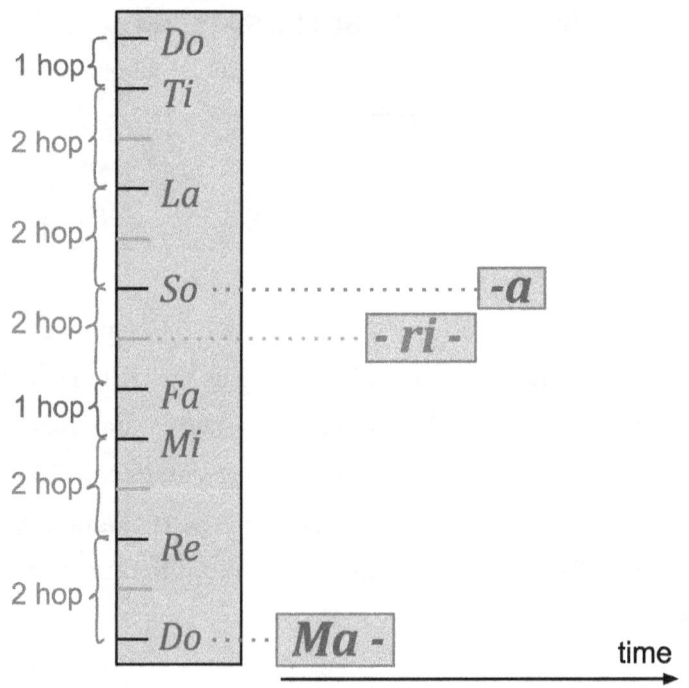

Tony does this to call special attention to the name of the beautiful woman he has just met.

Similarly, the opening theme for the TV show *The Simpsons* actually makes a quirky modification to the usual Major Scale throughout. The song is not in the major scale, but an unusual modified scale with the fourth note one semitone higher than it would be in the Major Scale and the seventh note one semitone lower than it would be in the Major Scale. This is a very uncommon scale; perhaps the Simpsons theme composer, Danny Elfman, did this just to warn us of the offbeat humor of *The Simpsons*:

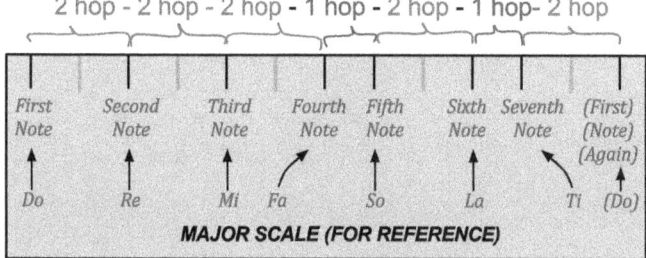

Scale Degrees

Let's say we're in a major scale, and we make up a tune that goes, *Do-Mi-Mi, Mi-So-So, Re-Fa-Fa, La-Ti-Ti* (as Sound of Music aficionados will know, Fraulein Maria has already made up this tune so that option's out if you're a budding composer, dear reader). Unless you're intimately familiar with the *Do-Re-Mi* system (also called **solfege**), it's hard to look at these notes and automatically internalise the ups and downs of this little tune -- how many hops are there between *Do* and *Mi*? is *Re* higher or lower than *So*? We could figure all of this out, of course, using the Major Scale diagram from a few pages ago, but it isn't intuitive or obvious at first glance.

But it becomes much easier for us to understand what the melody looks like if we label these notes with numerical values instead: *Do* = 1, *Re* = 2, *Mi* = 3, etc. Then the tune goes, 1-3-3, 3-5-5, 2-4-4, 6-7-7. Now we have a much better sense of the contours of the melody; it looks roughly like this:

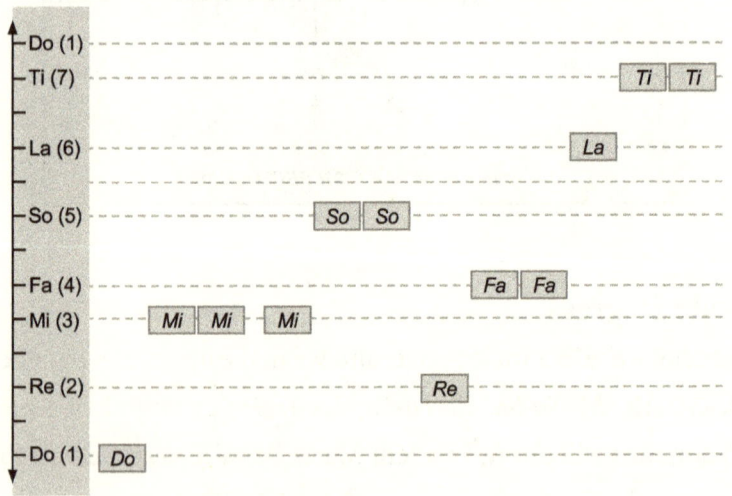

Thus, sometimes we name the notes of the scale by their **scale degrees**, that is, their position in the scale. In a Major Scale (using the movable *Do* system), *Do* is the first scale degree, *Re* is the second scale degree, *Mi* is the third, and so on. Similarly, we could refer to the notes of a pentatonic scale by their corresponding scale degrees, 1 through 5:

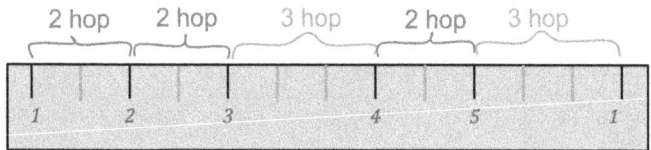

Defining the Gap

Scale degrees come in handy not only when we're identifying particular notes in the scale, but also when we're describing the distance between them. We could describe the distance between *Do* and *Re* as two semitones, and the distance between *Mi* and *Fa* as one semitone (as depicted in our Major Scale hop pattern). But when we're in a scale where we don't even use the semitone in between *Do* and *Re*, it is simpler to say that *Re* is one scale degree away from *Do*, and *Fa* is one scale degree away from *Mi*.

Musicians do have a naming system for the distances between scale degrees. A distance encompassing two scale degrees - e.g., the distance between *Do* and *Re*, or *Re* and *Mi* - is called a **second**.

A distance encompassing three scale degrees - e.g., the distance between *Do* and *Mi*, or *Mi* and *So* - is called a **third**, and so on.

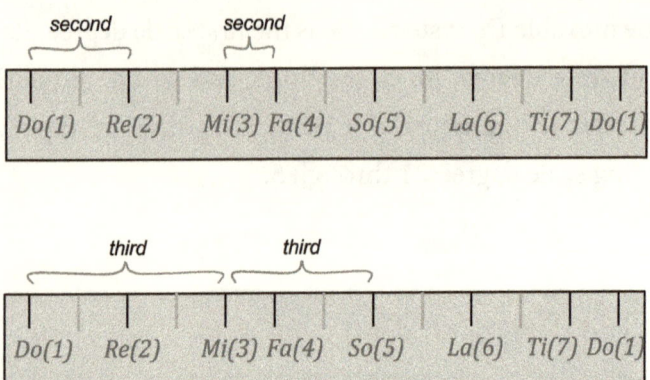

It does not escape musicians' notice that not all seconds are created equal, nor all thirds. If you take a careful look at the diagram above, depicting thirds, you'll notice that the first third (between *Do* and *Mi*) spans four semitones, while the second (between *Mi* and *So*) spans three. Musicians do have different names for these two types of thirds - a **major third** contains four semitones, while a **minor third** contains three.

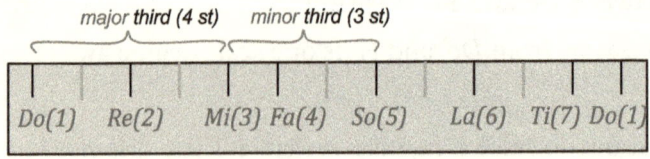

Similarly, if we look at the distance between *Do* and *Re*, and *Mi*

and *Fa*, we can see that the first distance spans two semitones, and the latter spans one:

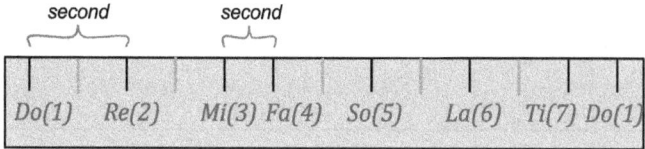

Thus, the first distance, two semitones, is called a **major second**, while the latter, one semitone, is called a **minor second**.

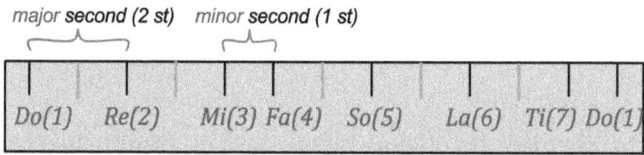

There are a few particular cases in which intervals are not described as "major" or "minor" but instead as "perfect," "augmented," and "diminished." The interval of a fifth, for example, is called a **perfect fifth** when it spans seven semitones, its most common form. This is because when two notes a perfect fifth apart are sounded together, they are thought to sound particularly - nay, perfectly - sonorous. A fifth spanning one semitone more than the perfect version is called an **augmented fifth**, while a fifth with one semitone fewer is called a **diminished fifth**. While there are no examples of an augmented fifth in the major or minor scale, there are examples of perfect and diminished fifths:

PERFECT FIFTHS:

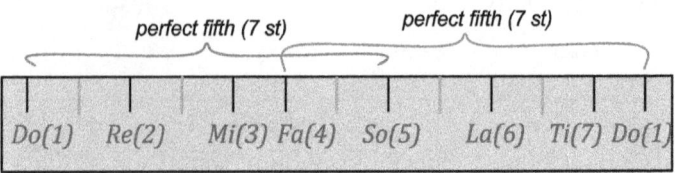

DIMINISHED FIFTH:

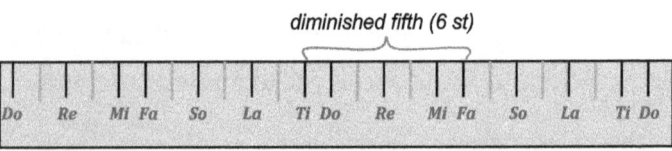

Fourths are also denoted as either perfect, diminished, or augmented. There are no diminished fourths in the Major or Minor Scales, but there are instances of perfect and augmented versions:

PERFECT FOURTHS:

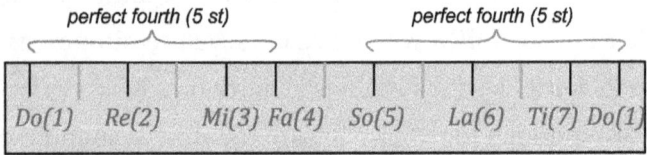

AUGMENTED FOURTH:

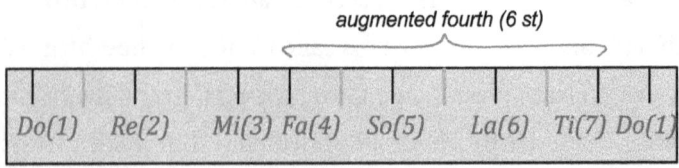

Notice any similarities between the diminished fifth and augmented fourth? They are both six semitones large, even though in one case they're four scale degrees apart and in the other they're five! There's nothing wrong with this; we can give intervals different names depending on how many scale degrees they encompass, even if they contain the same absolute number of semitones.

The six-semitone interval is also nicknamed the tritone, since it is three whole tones wide. (While we're on the subject, I should also let you know that two notes a tritone apart sound quite horrid together, so much so that this interval was famously called the *diabolus in musica* or "Devil in Music" in the Middle Ages!)

Finally, octaves are considered to be "perfect" intervals as well, since, as we've seen, they are gems of musical sonority. You could theoretically have diminished and augmented versions of an octave, though these don't make an appearance in the normal Major and Minor Scales.

Now, we've talked a lot about how intervals are named, but how does it sound when the two notes of an interval are played together? Therein lies the secret to making a marching band sound like a sharp outfit rather than an unpleasant clamor, and it is the subject of our next chapter.

Harmony

What's in a melody?

Most songs we listen to are composed of numerous interlocking parts, called **lines**. In a rock song, one line might be the lead guitar: throughout the song, there is a sequence of notes that the lead guitar plays. Another line might be the backup singers: they, too, have specific instructions for the notes they must sing (and the times they must sing them) in order to deliver their contribution to the overall song. The most prominent line in a song is called the **melody**. The melody is what we usually refer to as a song's *tune*: the most prominent featured line of sequential notes in the song. This is usually sung by the vocalist in most of the music we listen to today, or occasionally by other instruments when they have a "solo" within the music. The melody is the part of the song that you would sing to yourself in the shower (again, usually with words, but possibly with "dun-na-nunna-nun-na" noises for a particularly memorable guitar solo).

When overlapping lines of music are played at the same time, they create **harmony**: the use of simultaneous notes to create particular effects. For example, if we listen to a pop song, it's rare that the vocals and the electric guitar and the keyboard will all be playing the same note at the same time — instead, each of the instruments plays a note that complements the other notes being played at that moment to create a more pleasing effect overall.

If we imagine a song as an audible banquet, the *melody* would be the series of "main dishes" that are presented over time: first the soup, then the fish, then the meat, then the salad, then the cheese, then the dessert (except in music we're lucky enough to get *hundreds* of notes lined up in a single song — it's like having hundreds of dishes at a banquet). The *harmony*, meanwhile, would be the "pairings" that go with each of those courses to support and bring out the best in the starring items — for example, the carefully-chosen wines that complement each individual course on the menu. The harmony and the melody work together to create the overall experience of the song: the richness of music comes out of the way that melody and harmony interact to create something breathtaking.

Putting Two and Two Together

To understand harmony, let's first look at what happens when we pair two notes together. We're all used to hearing two notes sung simultaneously in duets. Think about your favorite duet – perhaps *Baby, It's Cold Outside*, or *A Whole New World* from the Disney film *Aladdin*. In both these songs, the singers sing luscious harmonies with each other each time the chorus appears.

For example, the harmonies in the chorus to *A Whole New World* look a little like this:

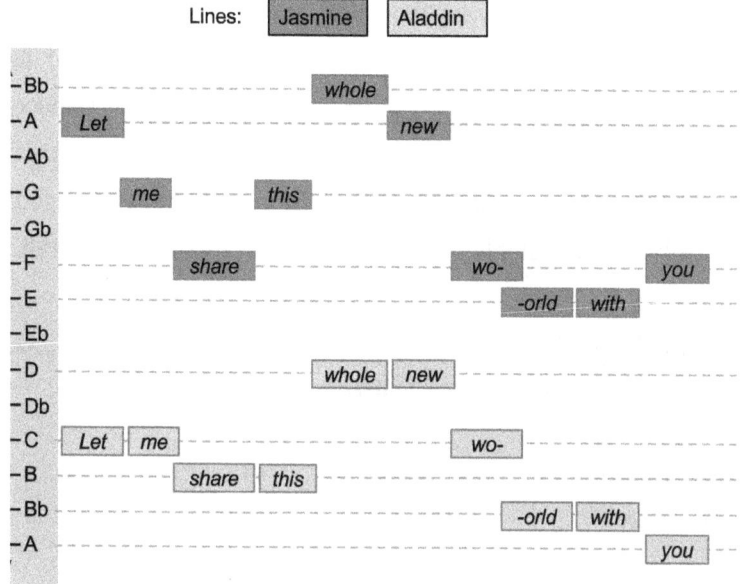

How do Aladdin and Jasmine get these harmonies to sound so good together? After all, when some of us are singing along to the radio, or at karaoke night, it doesn't come out sounding nearly so sweet.

Well, we can't simply put any two notes together and have them sound brilliant; just as we need to be choosy about the notes we use in our songs, we need to be choosy about how we put these notes together as well. What makes two notes sound pleasant or unpleasant together is the interval between them — i.e., how many semitones are in between. Certain intervals make the pairings sound stable, or **consonant**; others intervals sound unstable, or **dissonant**. When we're listening to music, our ears yearn to hear consonance, which feels satisfying and makes us breathe a sigh of happiness. While dissonant intervals are more unsettling, they aren't avoided altogether; rather, they're used to carefully and artfully lead us away from or toward consonance.

Here are the particular intervals that sound consonant vs. dissonant:

■ = dissonant intervals

Interval	Semitones	
Unison	0 semitones*	
Minor second	**1 semitone**	
Major second	**2 semitones**	
Minor third	3 semitones	
Major third	4 semitones	
Perfect fourth*	5 semitones	
Augmented fourth/ diminished fifth	**6 semitones**	
Perfect fifth	7 semitones	
Minor sixth	8 semitones	
Major sixth	9 semitones	
Minor seventh	**10 semitones**	
Major seventh	**11 semitones**	
Octave	12 semitones	

* There are certain musical contexts in which a five-semitone interval is considered dissonant.

While these rules may seem arbitrary at first, and while nobody knows *exactly* why we respond to these different intervals this way, there is one key pattern that could explain our instinctive responses to these different kinds of gaps: the frequency ratios between the notes in the consonant intervals are simpler than the frequency ratios between the notes of the dissonant intervals:

Consonant Intervals	Number of Semitones	Simple ratios
Unison	0 semitones	1:1
Minor third	3 semitones	6:5
Major third	4 semitones	5:4
Perfect fourth	5 semitones	4:3
Perfect fifth	7 semitones	3:2
Minor sixth	8 semitones	5:3
Major sixth	9 semitones	8:5
Octave	12 semitones	2:1

Dissonant Intervals	Number of Semitones	Complicated ratios
Minor second	1 semitone	16:15
Major second	2 semitone	10:9
Augmented fourth/ diminished fifth	6 semitones	64:45
Minor seventh	10 semitones	9:5
Major seventh	11 semitones	15:8

In terms of sound waves, this means that the peaks of the sound waves of the consonant intervals overlap more than the sound waves of the dissonant intervals. For example, let's look at the sound waves of two notes that are twelve semitones, or one octave, apart. The ratio of their frequencies is 2:1. This means that if the sound wave of the lower note looks like this:

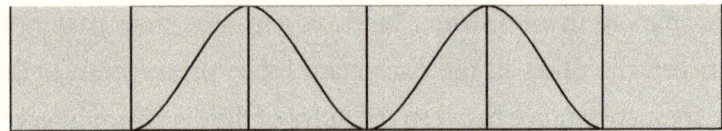

Then the sound wave of the higher note will look like this; it oscillates twice as frequently:

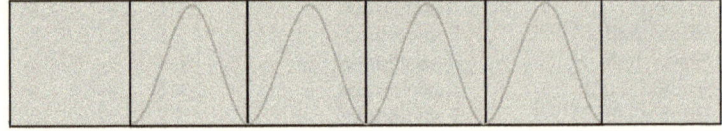

When the two notes are played together, their waves overlap like this:

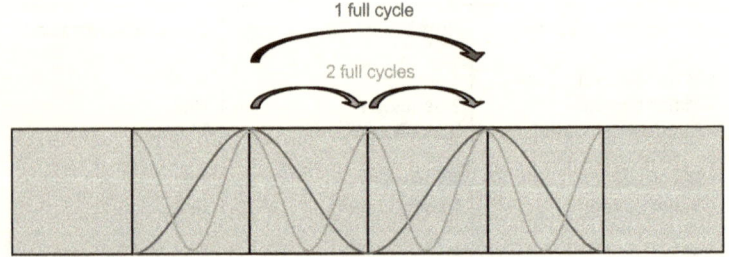

Since the higher note is twice the frequency of the lower note, it completes *two* full cycles for every *one* full cycle that the lower note completes; this is the definition of doubling the frequency of a wave. As a result, every peak in the wave of the lower note overlaps with every *second* peak in the wave of the higher note.

For a pair of notes a perfect fifth apart (a consonant interval), the frequency ratio is 3:2, and thus every third peak of one wave overlaps with every second peak of the other:

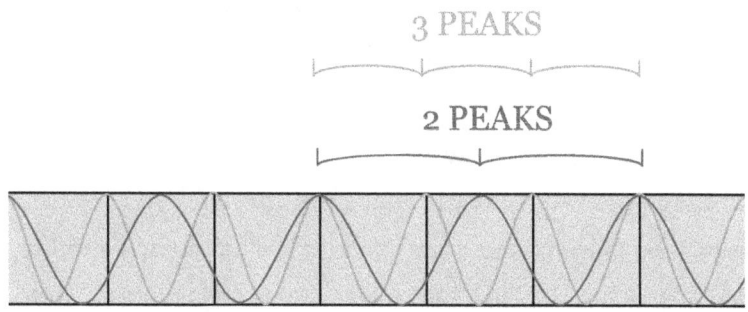

However, for a pair of notes that is a minor second apart (a dissonant interval), the frequency ratio is 16:15, so the wave-peaks overlap much less frequently — every 16th peak of one wave overlaps with every 15th of the other:

While no one really knows for sure, the difference between the "neat" pairs of waves that line up nicely with each other and the "messy" pairs that take a very long time to fall in sync may explain why some pairs of notes sound consonant to us and other pairs sound dissonant. Unfortunately, even if this "syncing" *is* the reason that some pairs of notes sound good together, no one yet knows for sure why synced-up waves would affect our brain so pleasantly.

Remember the one interval that we mentioned last chapter which stands out head and shoulders above the rest for its hideousness, the six-semitone "tritone"? Not coincidentally, its waves sync up the least out of all the intervals typically used in Western music.

Dissonant Intervals	Number of Semitones	Complicated ratios
Minor second	1 semitone	16:15
Major second	2 semitone	10:9
Augmented fourth/ diminished fifth	**6 semitones**	**64:45**
Minor seventh	10 semitones	9:5
Major seventh	11 semitones	15:8

When you move I move with you

Some things in life are just built to fit together, like Yin and

Thinking Musically Harmony

Yang, or peas and carrots. Certain intervals have a similar cosy relationship. Let's take our C Major Scale, for example, which uses the notes below:

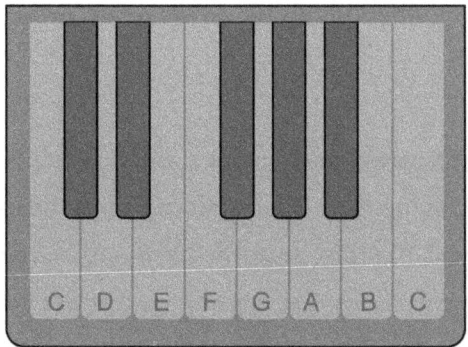

We might venture a guess that if we play a *C* and an *A* together then the combination will have a certain, similar sound whether we pair *A* with the lower *C* or with the higher *C*:

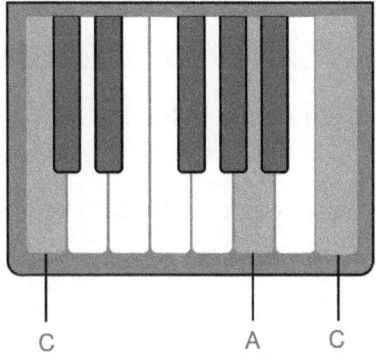

This is indeed correct. While the two pairs don't sound exactly the same — the one where the notes are closer together sounds tighter and has a warmer feeling than the one where the notes are further apart — they do have a very similar qualities. If each of these pairs were a color, they would likely come from the same set of tones; e.g., they'd both be earthy tones, or bright tones, or pastels.

To see how this might play out in song, let's return to Aladdin and Jasmine singing their duet. Jasmine sings the melody, starting on an *A*, and Aladdin sings the harmony, starting on a *C*:

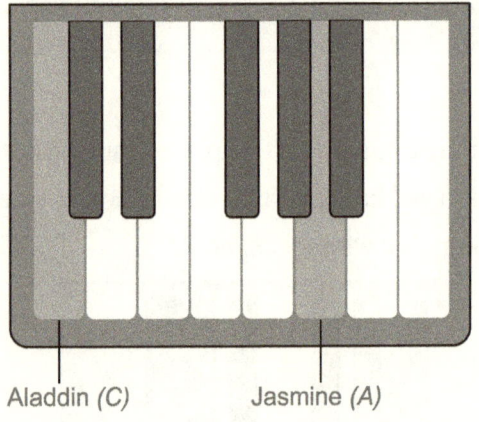

Aladdin *(C)*   Jasmine *(A)*

If they decide to switch parts — Aladdin wants to sing the tune, and Jasmine wants to sing the harmony — it'll be hard for Jasmine to sing Aladdin's part exactly, starting on the lower *C*, since Aladdin has a much lower voice. However, she can take the part up an octave and start it on the next *C* up, and we'll still hear the same harmonies as we heard when Aladdin was an octave lower.

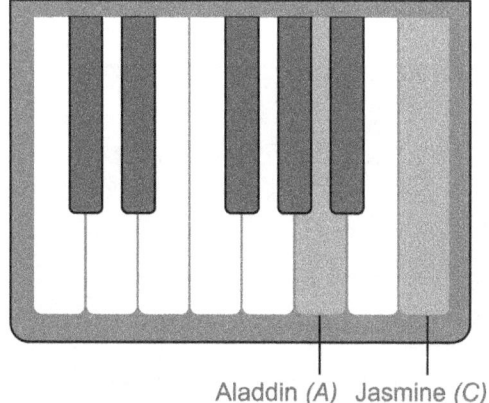

Aladdin *(A)*   Jasmine *(C)*

Therefore, it makes sense that *C-A* pairs sound similar, regardless of which note is on the top or the bottom. The implication is that almost of all of our pitch-pairs have complements that sound very similar. Let's take a look at our *C-A* pair first. As we saw, we can make a *C-A* pair with a major sixth (nine semitones):

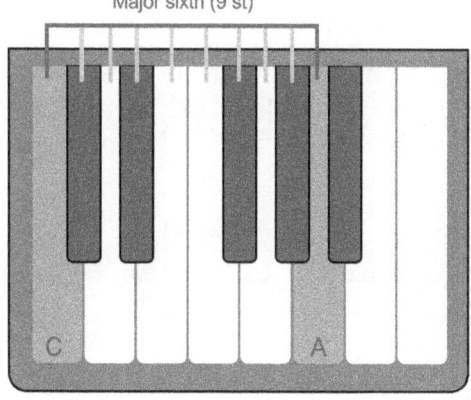

Or with a minor third (three semitones):

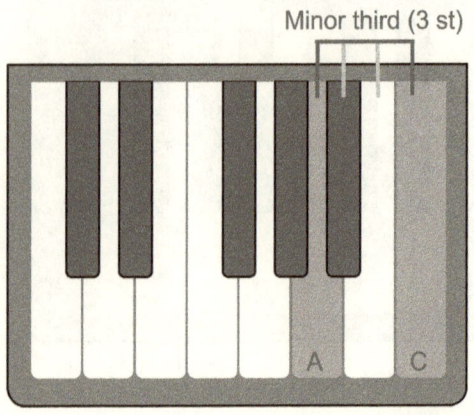

Thus, a major sixth sounds qualitatively similar to a minor third. Note that the two complements, naturally, add up to 12 semitones, the octave:

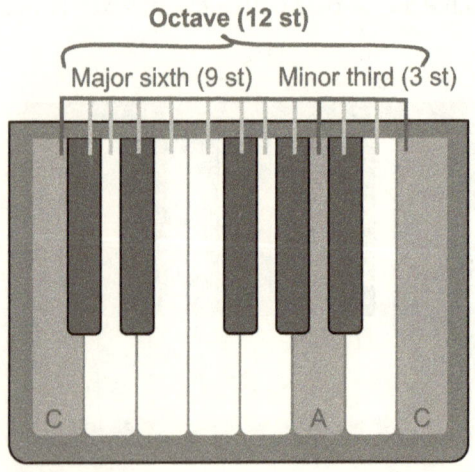

This is true of any pair of complements: a particular pitch-pair and its complement add up to an octave. We call these complements **inversions**; here are the pairs of inversions:

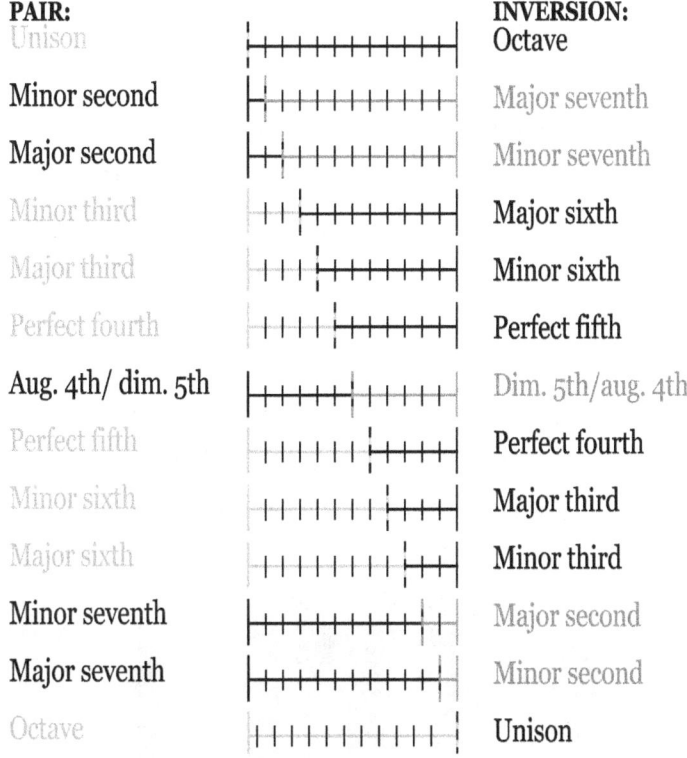

Note that the tritone, the dreaded six-semitone pair, is its own inversion (since six and six make twelve), and this is probably rather a good thing, as we don't want to hear too much of that kind of sound anyway!

Three's company

Imagine you're hanging out with a good friend, someone you really get along with, just having a nice chat. You go well together — one could even say you *complement* each other. Suddenly, a third person walks into the room. If you both like this new arrival then the conversation might get even better — there is something rich and satisfying about three good friends all playing off each other. But if one of you doesn't get along with the new arrival then a definite feeling of dissonance will probably start to arise. Unsurprisingly, the same applies to musical notes. We call a group of three or more notes a **chord**.

If we put three notes together in such a way that all the intervals between the pairs of notes are consonant, then the *three* notes together will sound consonant as well. Let's take a look at a *C-E-G* chord, for example:

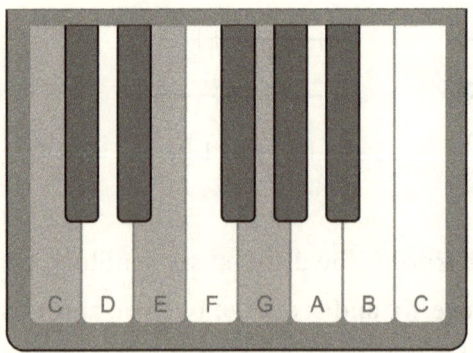

This chord consists of entirely consonant intervals; a major third, a minor third, and a perfect fifth (we abbreviate major third as "**M3**," minor third as "**m3**," and perfect fifth as "**P5**"):

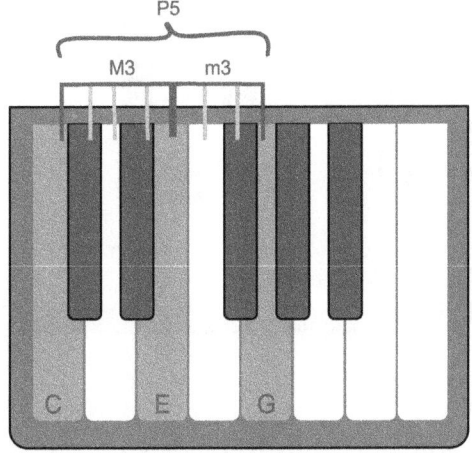

Any chord with three notes spaced like this — with a major third and then a minor third — sounds qualitatively happy, and we call it a **major chord**. (Musicians think of these intervals as being stacked on top of each other vertically, as they are when the chord is written on a sheet of music, so we can think of the major third as being *beneath* the minor third). By contrast, a chord like the one below, with a minor third beneath a major third, sounds qualitatively sad (while still sounding perfectly consonant), and we call it a **minor chord**:

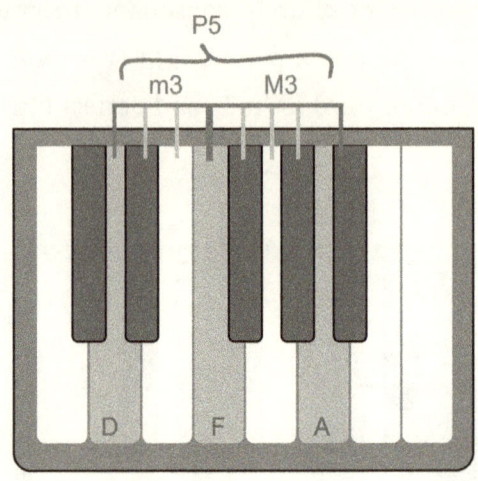

Why these chords make us feel happy or sad, no one knows; some posit it has to do with our brain chemistry, and some posit that it's culturally ingrained in Western music. As these things usually go, it may well be a complicated combination of both.

Note that we can take any of the intervals in the major chord, replace it with its inversion, and it will still sound qualitatively the same, though the notes will sound a bit more distant from each other rather than sounding as tight as in the first version of the chord we introduced. So, for example, here we have the same notes (*C*, *E*, and *G*) but with a *C* on top rather than on the bottom of the chord:

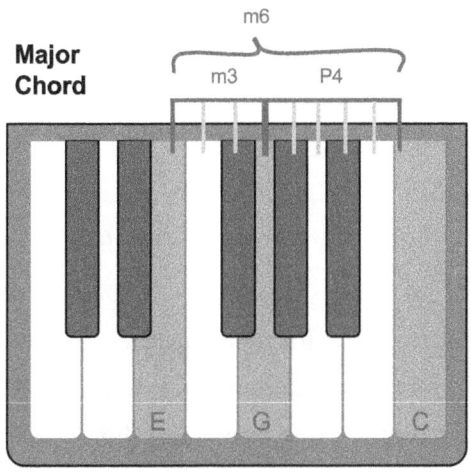

And here we have the same three notes *again* but with the G on the bottom instead of on top:

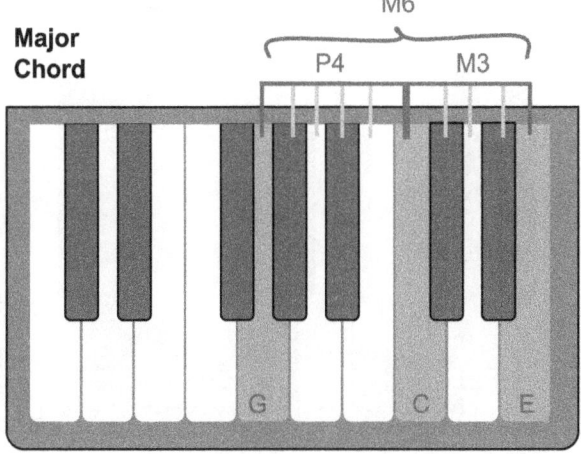

In all of these cases, every single interval involved is consonant — if you don't believe us you can check on the chart we drew a few pages back! This is quite spectacular, when you think about it: so long as we pick the right groups of notes, we can combine them in whatever we way we like and come out with something that sounds qualitatively the same.

The same idea holds true for minor chords: once again, minor chords sound "sad" to us but they still sound *consonant*; they sound sad in a way that fits well together. Earlier we gave the example of the minor chord using *D*, *F* and *A*, in that order. But we could also play the same chord in other ways; for example, by putting the *D* on top:

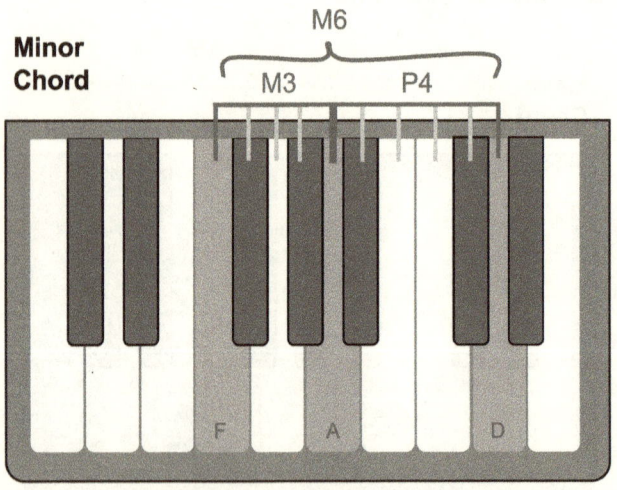

Or, similarly, we could play the same notes but with the *F* on top, giving us this:

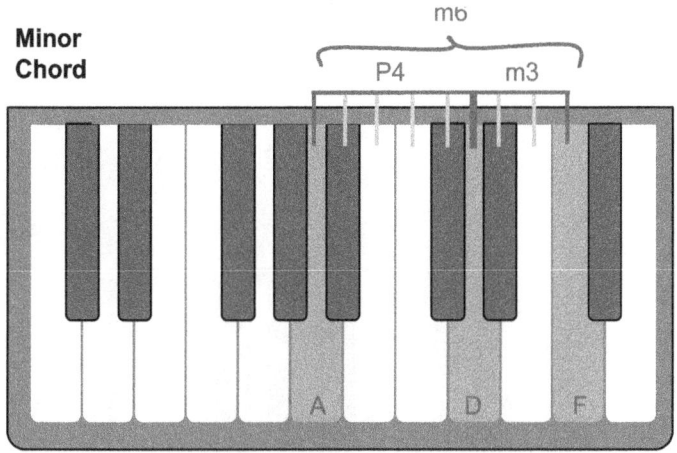

When we take the most basic form of a chord — in the case of major and minor chords, the "tightest" version of these chords where the notes are as close together as possible — and then we take the bottom note and move it elsewhere in the chord, we refer to this as an **inversion** of the basic form (it's the same idea as the inversion of a pair of notes that we saw earlier).

Four's a crowd

A short while ago we were imagining sitting in a room with one friend when, all of a sudden, a new addition walked in. If the new person meshed well with both of the original conversants then suddenly we had a chord: an even richer combination, with deep harmonies between all the participants. Now: what would happen if a fourth person walked into the room and started talking?

In music, as soon as we add a fourth note to a chord, we inevitably – yes, inevitably! – introduce a dissonant interval within the chord. Take a look at our major *C-E-G* chord below:

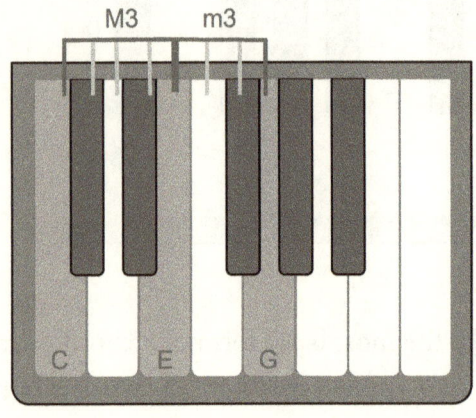

If we're in a C Major Scale, adding any of the other notes of the scale adds a dissonance:

- *D* creates a dissonant major second with *C* and *E*
- *F* creates a dissonant minor second with *E* and a dissonant major second with *G*
- *A* creates a dissonant major second with *G*
- *B* creates a dissonant major seventh with *C*

While adding an extra note might add a dissonant interval to a chord, the presence of consonant intervals as well often makes the chord sound interesting, with a particular strange color to it, but not as unstable as a dissonant interval played alone. In the same way that two people who don't get along would probably never hang out together, because then there would be nothing but unpleasant dissonance, perhaps there are occasions where four people spend time together and one pair among them actually have a bit of discord between them; perhaps it adds an interesting element of drama, an alternative viewpoint, and certainly a different tone to an otherwise completely consonant conversation. Chords with four or more notes have a variety of different colors; some sound cautious and make us feel like we're in limbo; others sound very discordant and make us cringe, while still others sound quite suave. While these chords don't feel quite as stable as consonant three-note chords, they do add a wide variety of colors to the musical palette.

Chords in Song

As we mentioned at the start of the chapter, harmonies are created in a song through the overlap of a tune with several other lines played simultaneously—maybe a back-up singer, guitar, and keyboard. All of the notes played simultaneously across all of the lines at any given point in time create a chord.

While we may be familiar with an electric guitar or a keyboard banging out chords beneath the vocals, the notes sung by your favorite singer must also contain notes of the chords played beneath her in order for the melody to sound harmonious with the underlying musical texture.

The chords used in a song use the notes of the scale that is used in the song (except for cases where an out-of-scale note is added for artistic flair). We can construct basic, three-note chords built on each of the notes of the scale that we're in. Let's again take a look at our C Major Scale; the C Major Scale contains all of the following chords, one starting on each note of the scale:

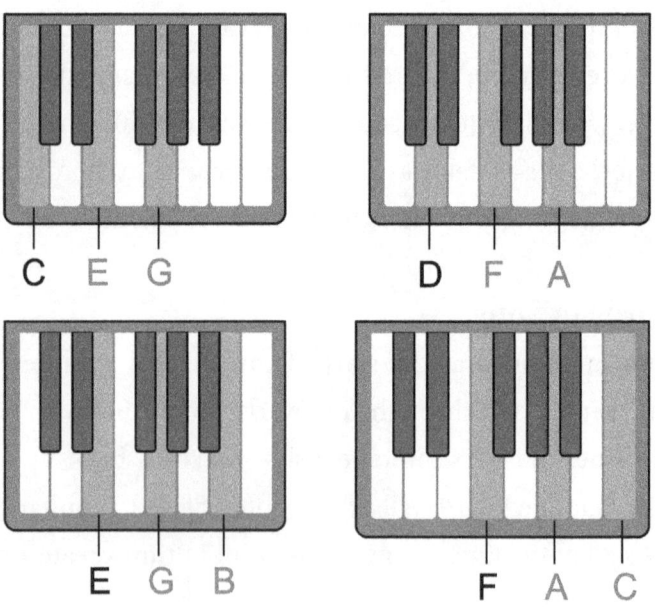

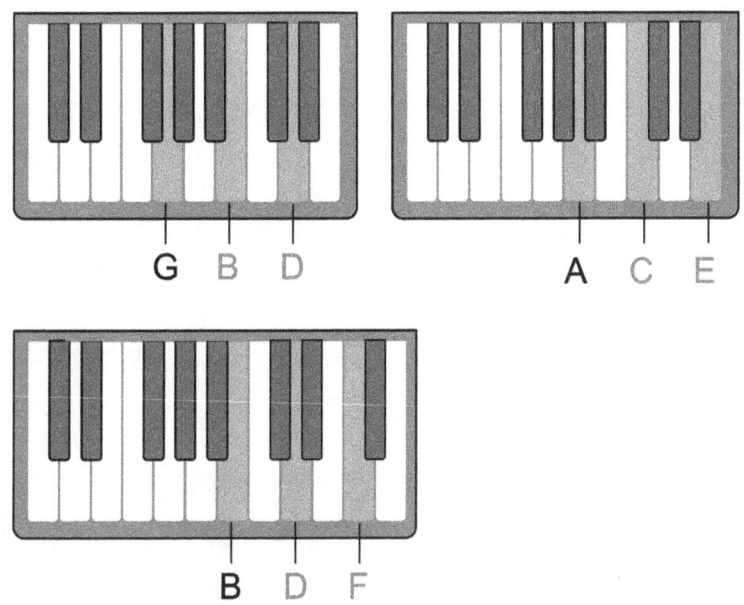

Some of the chords are major, and some are minor — remember, a major chord is a *major* third (four semitones) beneath a *minor* third (three semitones), whereas a minor chord is a *minor* third (three semitones) beneath a *major* third (four semitones).

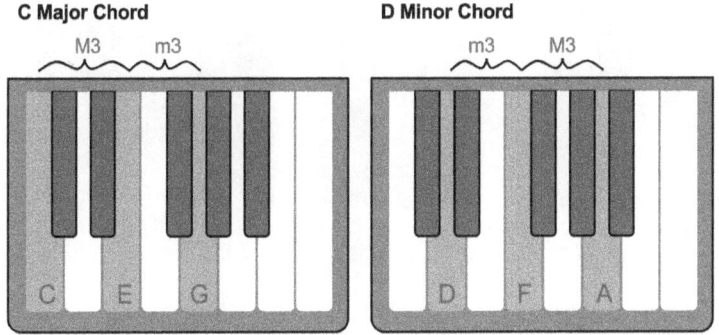

E Minor Chord

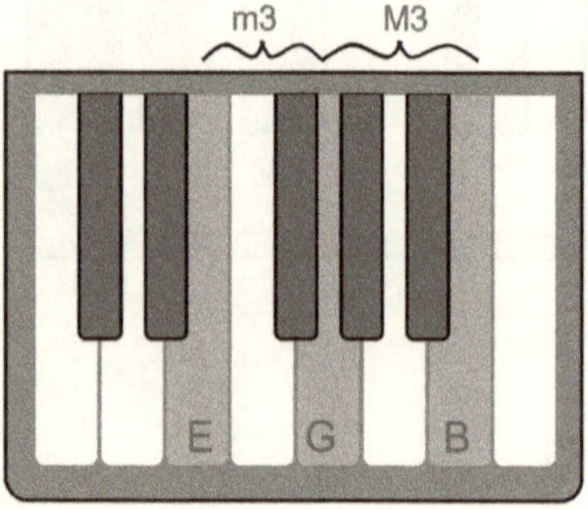

F Major Chord

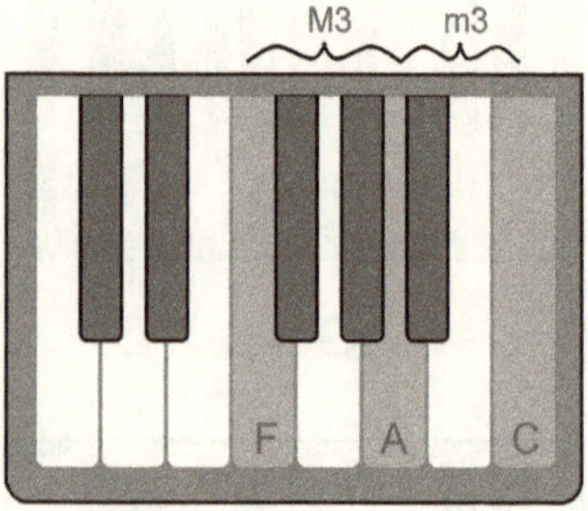

G Major Chord

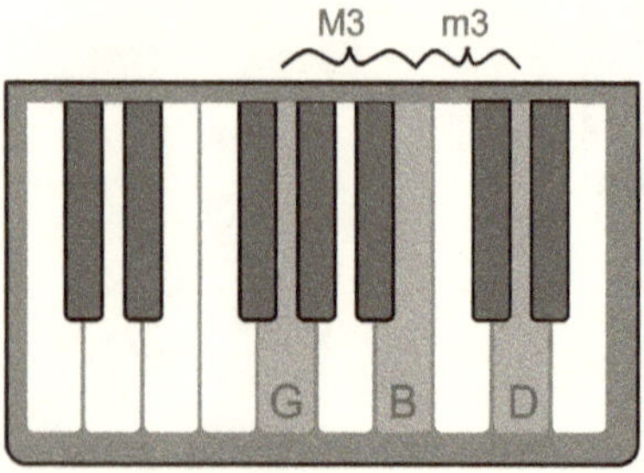

A Minor Chord

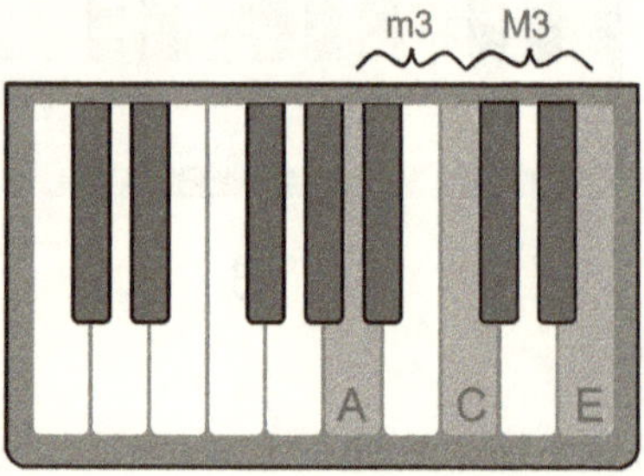

But one of these chords is a rebel:

B Diminished Chord

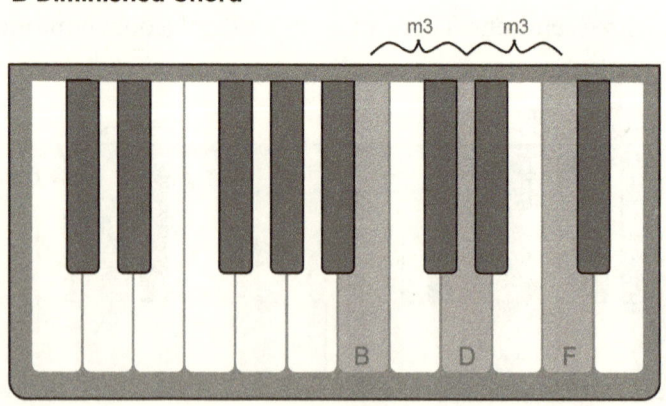

The chord built on the seventh note of a major scale (in our case *B*, which is the seventh note in the C Major Scale) is neither major nor minor. Nor is it built entirely of consonant intervals; unlike our previous chords that consisted of consonant minor thirds, major thirds, and perfect fifths, this one contains our six-semitone tritone:

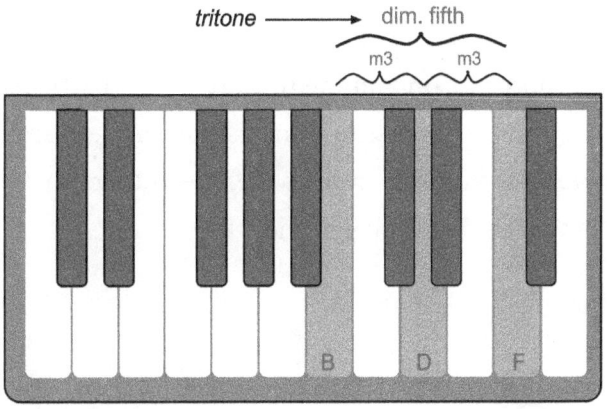

We call it a **diminished chord**: a chord made up of a minor third stacked on top of another minor third.

We can conveniently name each of these chords by the note of the scale it starts on. We can even do this in a generalised fashion, so that we can identify the underlying chord patterns among pieces of music regardless of which scale we're using. As such, we use uppercase Roman numerals for the major chords and lowercase Roman numerals for the minor chords to identify chords without reference to the particular scale we're in. The chord starting on the first note of the Major Scale (which is a major chord) is a *I* chord, and the chord starting on the second note of the Major Scale (which is a minor chord) is a *ii* chord. Whether or not a particular chord comes out as major or minor just depends on which notes are included in the scale, and the intervals between them: the composer doesn't "decide" whether, say, the chord starting on the third note of a particular scale is major or minor, because (as long as she isn't artistically adding in a note that is outside of the scale) the notes of that particular scale have already decided for her:

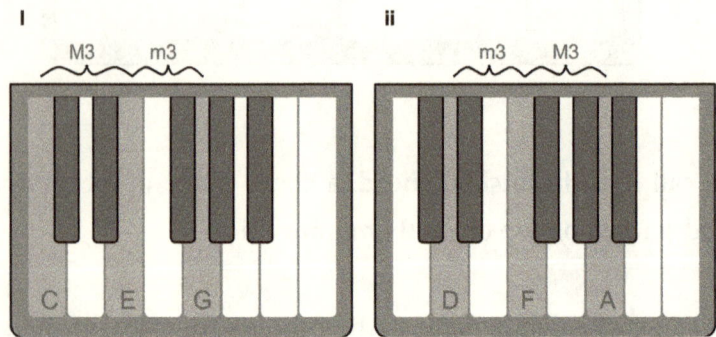

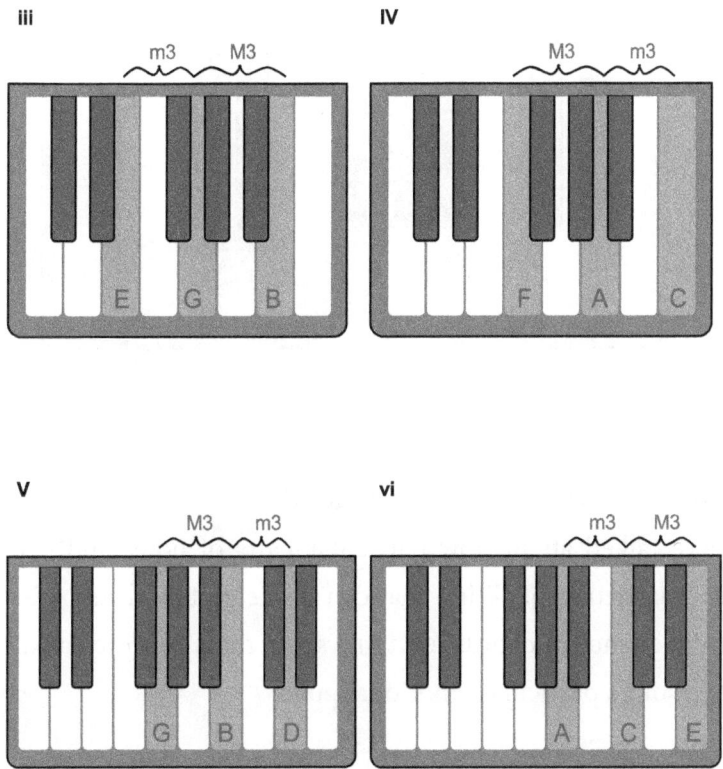

The chord built on the seventh note of the Major Scale is causing problems for us again — it's neither major nor minor, so it's denoted with lowercase Roman numerals and gets its own special symbol to show us that it's diminished:

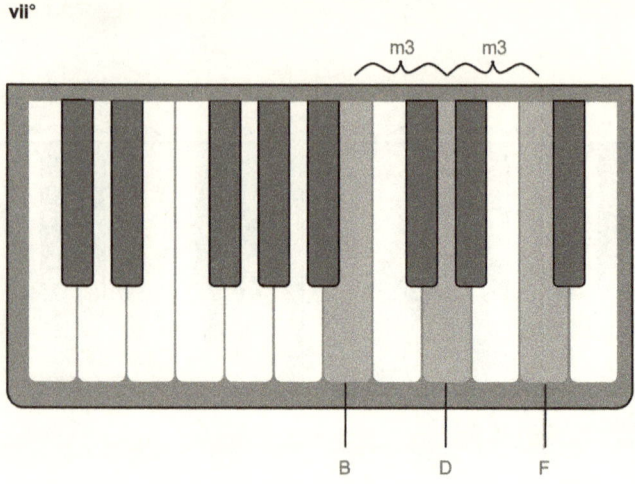

Moving From Chord To Chord

We've talked about how particular pairs of notes and chords have particular qualities, that can evoke certain feelings in us. The sequence of chords used in a song, then, sets the backdrop for a song's particular emotional pull.

A chord sequence is also called a **chord progression**. Throughout a song, the sequence of chords used will often start on the chord built on the first note of the scale, wander away from it, and then back toward it over some period of time. While we might not always be consciously aware of this as we're listening to music, we can actually *feel* a certain instability as we move away from the chord built on the first note of the scale and a sense of "relief" when we get back to it later.

For example, let's look at the song *Ain't No Sunshine*, by Bill Withers. As Bill's voice soars on the words:

Ain't no sun-shine when she's go-one
And she's always gone too long
Any time she goes away

We feel a palpable sense of giddiness, as if the music were taking us on a roller coaster ride. But there is also a sense of unresolved instability. If you have a recording of this song handy — there are many versions available online — try the following exercise: skip to the part towards the middle of the song where Bill sings the lines above, and hit "pause" exactly after he sings "gone too long." You should feel a very strange, completely palpable sense that something is "wrong" — this is just not a place where the song can stop. Something in your mind feels unfinished and unresolved. Then press "play" again and pause the song again after the subsequent line: "any time she goes away." Suddenly, everything feels fine — although you are still stopping in the middle of the song, this now feels like a point in the music where it is okay to stop. There are, of course, a number of factors contributing to this effect — for example, in one case you are stopping in the middle of a sentence, which probably confuses your brain as well, but the underlying chord progression is also confusing you in the sense that one of these stopping points has left you teetering on the brink; it's actually left you on a chord built on the fourth note of the scale, yearning to go back to the chord built on the first note of the scale. Musicians use the terms **tension** and **resolution** to describe this phenomenon: the way that, within any chord progression, some chords create a tension inside us that isn't resolved until we get back to a more stable chord.

A typical chord progression might go: *I, vi, IV, V, I, IV, V, I* — it starts on *I*, the chord built on the first note of the scale, and periodically gets back to *I* again. A particular chord typically underlies a few words of one line of lyrics; one line of the lyrics might have two or three sequential chords beneath it. The melody will typically contain one or more of the notes in the chord beneath it, and perhaps some notes that are outside of the chord as well but are fleeting enough that our ears register the harmonies.

Even if a tune contains many different notes of the scale, bear in mind that this doesn't necessarily mean that there need to be many different chords beneath it to create nice harmonies. Rather, since each chord contains three notes of the scale, it only takes three chords to cover all notes of the scale (there are seven notes in the scale, and three chords with three notes each gives us nine notes, so we've already covered the entire scale and repeated some of the notes as well). Hence, many rock or pop songs can be played using just four chords, usually the following four: I, IV, V, vi.

While the chords I, IV, and V would suffice to encompass all the notes in the scale, they are all major chords; the minor chord starting on the sixth note of the scale adds a little extra color - and tension - to the harmony, so the music doesn't just use a chord with one particular color the whole time. That said, there are still some (pretty happy) songs built on just the I, IV, and V chords!

You may be wondering why these particular four chords are chosen — there are plenty of other chords that are also "allowed" in the scale, so why did these ones come to dominate the music we listen to? We mentioned that some chords feel more stable to us than others; the three chords I, IV and V best "define" the scale and give us a feeling of stability within it, hence they're the most commonly used in popular music. Some other random sequence of chords — say, iii - ii - vi - IV — would throw the listeners off completely.

Let's take a look at *Take Me Home, Country Roads* as an example; the song uses the following chords in the verse:

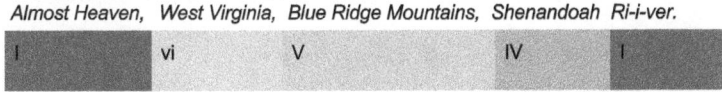

The same chords repeat for each line of the verse, as the tune stays virtually the same. Then the tune changes for the chorus, as does the chord progression beneath it:

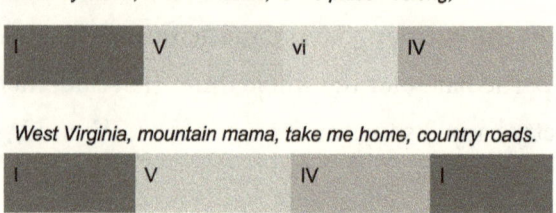

In songs with bridges, typically the bridge will have yet another chord progression beneath it as the tune changes yet again.

Chord progressions can play a role in defining different types of music as well. In blues, one standard chord progression is the following twelve-chord progression (in which each chord is played for the same length of time). We're familiar with it from the verses of *Hound Dog* by Elvis Presley, each of which follows this progression:

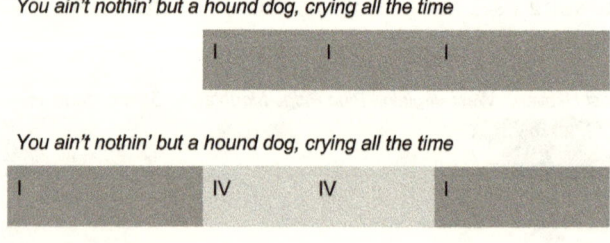

Well, you ain't never caught a rabbit and you ain't no friend of mine

| I | V | IV | I | I |

Many blues melodies — standard and improvised — can be constructed on top of this simple twelve-chord sequence.

It may be perplexing that so many songs can be built off of so very few chords. But it also tells us that even using just a few chords there is a lot of room for experimentation with melody, harmony, rhythm, and beat — which brings us to our next chapter.

Rhythm & Beat

We've talked a lot about how notes make up music. But it isn't just the notes that make us want to tap our feet or clap our hands as we listen to Billy Joel at a piano bar, or to Ke$ha at a dance club, or to One Direction at any time or place — it's also the catchy rhythms and beat!

In any given tune, not all notes are of equal duration; we know that some notes are held for longer than others. Let's take the chorus of *Livin' on a Prayer* by Bon Jovi, for example:

Whooooooa, we're halfway theeere,
Whooooa! Livin' on a prayer
Take my hand, we'll make it, I swear,
Whooooa! Livin' on a prayer

The "Whooooa"'s are much longer than the rest of the words in the chorus; indeed, that's why we love singing them! There's also a bit of a space between "Whooooa!" and "Livin' on a prayer," in which we catch our breath. All tunes have a pattern of longer and shorter notes and silences. **Rhythm** is what we call the pattern of duration of notes (and silences) in a particular line of music. The rhythm of the music we listen to is rather complex, since each line of music has its own rhythm. A singer's melody, a guitar's riff, and a bass guitar's ambling line don't move from note to note all at the same time; yet, their lines all seem to consistently sync up to create recognizable, catchy music! We know that the notes in these lines are all in harmony, but how do they all fit together in time?

Let's first look at the rhythm of a simple tune. We know that certain notes in any tune sound longer than others. For example, in the first lines of the chorus of *Jingle Bells*, "bells," "all," and "way" sound particularly long:

Jingle beeells, Jingle beeells
Jingle aaall the waaay!

In fact, if we say the length of the word "bells" is one unit, this is precisely how long each note is relative to "bells":

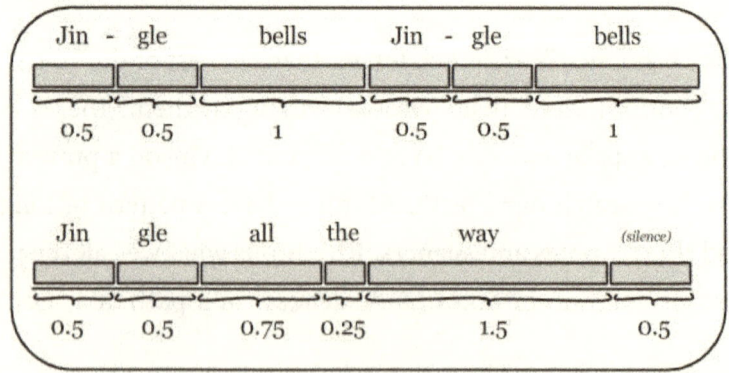

Indeed, relative to the length of "bells," each syllable of "Jingle" is only 0.5 units long, while "way" is a whole 1.5 units long!

The "unit of time" used in a particular song is called its **beat**. So if "bells" is one beat long, then each syllable of "Jingle" is 0.5 beats long, and "way" is 1.5 beats long. At the end of the line, there is a 0.5-beat silence, basically so we can catch our breath before we proceed with the following line.

You may be asking, "why did we decide that *bells* is one beat long and that the lengths of the other notes would be measured relative to *bells*?" Well, we can't just pick any unit of time in a given song to designate as the beat; the beat also provides an underlying pulse for a piece of music to which all rhythms are tied. Starting at the beginning of the song, the beat strikes at regular intervals in time, like the tick-tock of your clock or the sound of your boot hitting the pavement each step when you walk at a steady pace.

For example, if your friend Jonathan wanted to sing *Jingle Bells*, and your friend Aditya happened to have a tambourine on hand, Aditya might tap the tambourine along to Jonathan's *Jingle Bells* chorus thus:

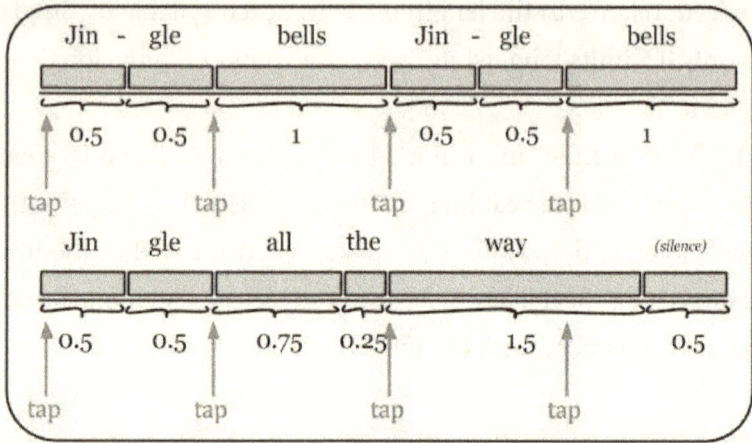

This would result in a very pleasing accompaniment to Jonathan's vocals; we would feel that Aditya is tapping along with the natural beat of the melody.

The next time the chorus appears, Aditya could tap his tambourine twice as fast as he did the first time, and we would still feel that he is providing a pleasing accompaniment to the melody:

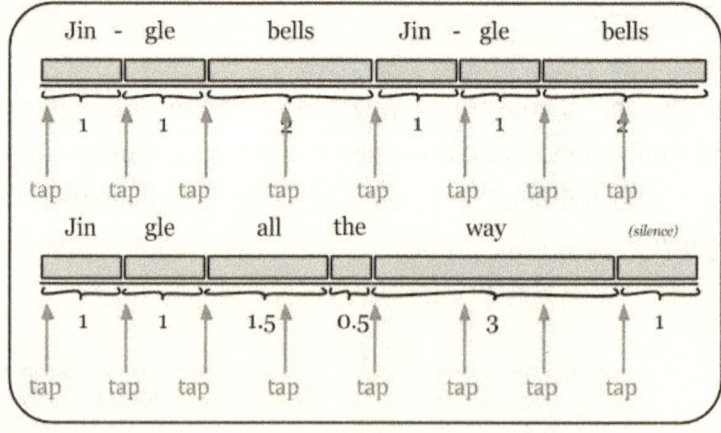

On the other hand, if Aditya tapped the tambourine as denoted below, three times for every instance of "Jingle bells," it would throw Jonathan (and his listeners) off, because he'd now be articulating a pulse different from the natural pulse of the melody. These new beats only align with "Jin-" and "way," whereas in the previous examples the beat had struck on "Jin-," "bells," and sometimes "-gle" as well:

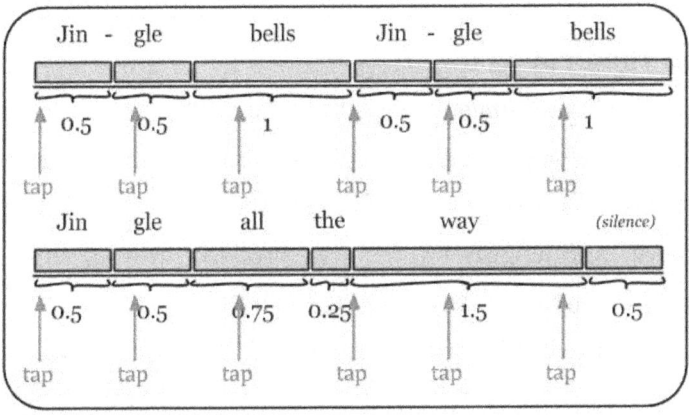

While this might be a fun prank for Aditya, the listener would feel like he was off from the natural beat of the melody.

Like in *Jingle Bells*, most music has a natural beat that goes with it, usually aligned to the most basic note-length in the melody (or prominent harmonic lines) and simple subdivisions or multiples thereof. You may wonder how we choose among these subdivisions and multiples of note-lengths; often, the beat that feels most natural to us is the one that the music naturally emphasizes (e.g., through tambourine-taps or drum hits as we saw above, or even through the timing of shifts from one chord to another or of accented syllables in the lyrics). It's also usually a length to which we can naturally tap our feet, clap our hands, nod our heads, tap a tambourine, or execute whatever bodily movements we desire — not too slow, not too fast!

Feel the Beat

If you're singing *Jingle Bells* without Aditya by your side to tap a tambourine by your ear, you may not be able to tap out the pulse of the beat yourself even if you sing the tune with all the right relative note-lengths (which you probably would, since you hear this song incessantly during the holidays). Indeed, the beat is sometimes hidden in a song; you can hear it in the bass drum and snare drum if you keep an ear out for it, but they sound like a speck in the musical landscape of your favorite song. While finding the beat can be easy for a musician or a dancer, it can be trying for the rest of us as we tune in to the vocals.

There are a few instances, however, in which the beat is very prominent, as those who listen to Queen can attest. In *We Will Rock You*, the stomp-stomp-clap rhythm very clearly shows us where the beat is. Here's the rhythm of the chorus:

Thinking Musically Rhythm & Beat

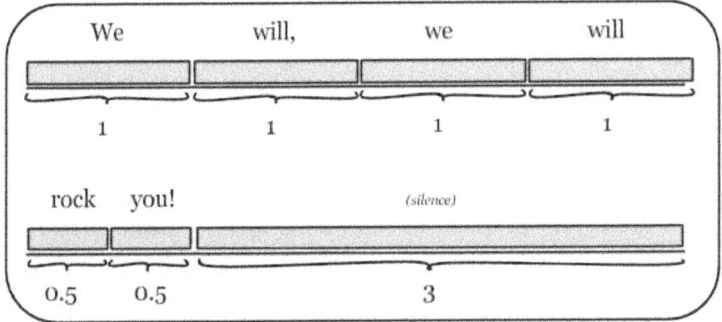

The stomp-stomp-clap's that accompany the chorus occur in a half-beat, half-beat, full-beat pattern like so:

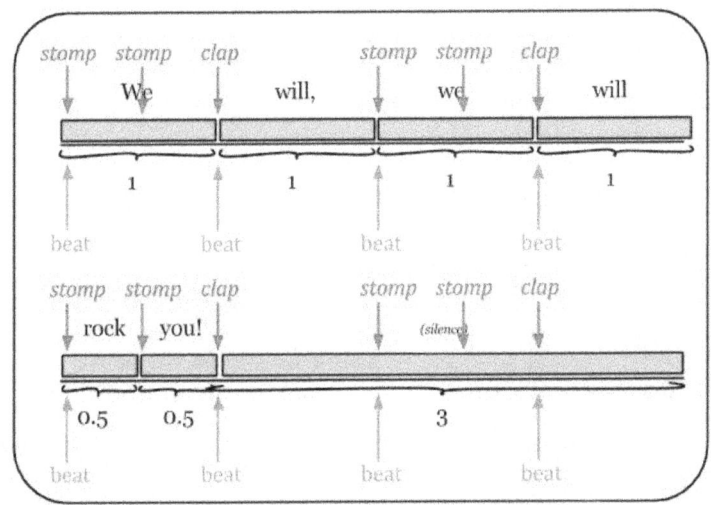

Here, you can hear the beat on the first "stomp" and the "clap" of each stomp-stomp-clap sequence. While it may be easy to stomp-stomp-clap in rhythm with the beat in *We Will Rock You*, in many other songs the rhythmic patterns in each line of music make it hard to find the beat. However, you should know that there still is a beat underlying almost all music you listen to!

There are a few instances in which music doesn't contain a regular underlying pulse at all. Some religious chants may have a discernible rhythm — words are held for different durations — but no regular beat underlying the chant's rhythm. In some opera, there are sections that are meant to sound more like speech than like song; in these sections, how long notes are held is largely at the singer's discretion, and there is no regular beat. Songs in musicals sometimes start with a semi-sung, semi-spoken segment without a regular beat, such as the beginnings of the songs *For Good* or *Defying Gravity* from Wicked. The music that we dance to in clubs, on the other hand, definitely contains a regular beat that we gyrate to.

Tempo

We all know that a song can be sung faster or slower depending on the person who's singing it. Indeed, Americans most commonly experience this with the American national anthem. *The Star-Spangled Banner* is sung at the start of major sporting events and, depending on the singer, can speed past merrily (so we can get to the game) or march with solemn slowness.

Though musicians playing a piece will sometimes take liberties with how fast they play a song (witness those national anthem singers who take whatever time they feel like), composers often tell musicians how fast a piece of music should go. We call the speed of a song its **tempo**. In the same way that we might talk about the speed of a car (in miles per hour), we can define the speed of a song in *beats per minute*. If the composer wants a tune to be played quickly then she will tell the musicians to use a lot of beats per minute; each beat will then be quite short, and the tune as a whole will move forward more briskly. If the composer wants a tune to be played slowly, she will tell the musicians to use few beats per minute; each beat will then be quite long, and the tune as a whole will move more slowly.

You may already be familiar with the beats per minute unit if you were ever taught to measure your heart rate in grade school. There, you found out that if you put your hand on your heart, set a timer for one minute, and counted how many times your heart beat before the timer went off, you would know your heart rate — perhaps 60 beats per minute (bpm) if you're a trained athlete, or 85 beats per minute if you're a non-athletic writer. If your heart rate was slower, e.g., 60 bpm, that meant that there was a 1 second lapse between beats. If it was higher, e.g., 85 bpm, then each beat came more quickly, every ~0.706 seconds.

If you're wondering how musicians can tell how fast to play when they see the 85 bpm indication at the top of a piece of music (are they just incredibly good at calculating tempo in their heads?), they use a nifty little tool called a **metronome**. On a metronome, a musician can input the desired tempo in beats per minute, and the metronome taps out the beats. Traditional metronomes had a pendulum that would sway to the beat at the desired speed, though modern digital metronomes just make a loud ticking noise on each beat. Once a musician practices a piece a few times, they usually know the tempo, just as you internalize the tempo of songs like *Jingle Bells* after hearing them once or twice.

Musical Phrases

In many of the poems we know, each line takes about the same amount of time for us to say. Let's take the nursery rhyme *Humpty Dumpty*, for example:

Humpty Dumpty sat on a wall,
Humpty Dumpty had a great fall.
All the king's horses and all the king's men,
Couldn't put Humpty together again.

While the third line might take slightly more time than the others because it has more words, each line takes about the same amount of time to say. The rhyming syllables "fall," "wall," "men," and "-gain" occur at approximately equal intervals. Musical lyrics also tend to take about the same amount of time to say per line too, as in *Jingle Bells*:

Jingle bells, jingle bells,
Jingle all the way.
Oh, what fun it is to ride
In a one-horse open sleigh!

There could be slight variation in the lengths of each line when we speak the lyrics to *Jingle Bells*. However, when these words are set to music, the lines fall into a regular pattern of an average of four beats per line:

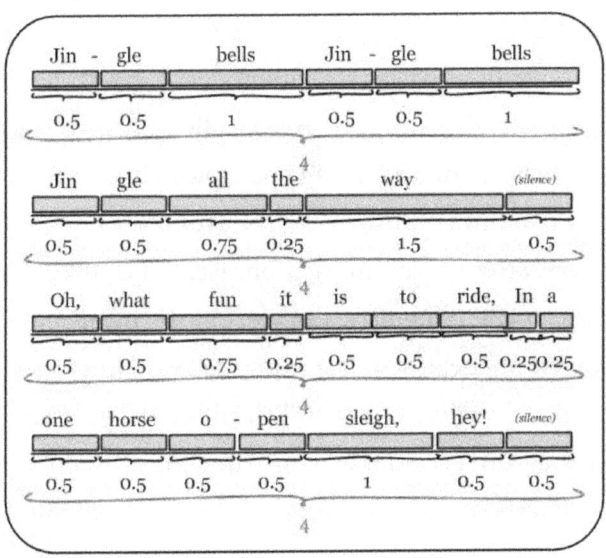

(You may have noticed that at the end, "Oh what fun it is to ride" takes up 3.5 beats, while "In a one horse open sleigh, hey!" takes up 4.5 beats. It's quite common for lines of lyrics to borrow and steal a few beats from each other, as long as each line comes out to an equal number of beats on *average*.)

In most music we listen to, each line of lyrics takes up the same number of beats on average, which helps lend structure to the song. In Jingle Bells, each line takes up four beats; this recurring pattern gets us into the groove of the music, while the variation in the notes and lyrics used in each line keeps our interest the whole way through!

In almost all music — not just popular music with lyrics, but also classical music, jazz, and even music across cultures — songs can be divided into segments each characterized by a distinct, discernible musical shape, called **phrases**. In popular music, a musical phrase typically occupies a line or two of lyrics, like every two lines of Jingle Bells, or every two lines in the chorus of *Livin' on a Prayer*. In each phrase, not only do the words themselves form a linguistic phrase, but the music also forms a recognizable shape: if you just hum the line, "Jingle bells, jingle bells, jingle all the way" any child will recognize it and be able to name that tune! (And if you hum the lines "Whoa, we're halfway there; Whoa! Livin' on a Prayer" from *Livin' on a Prayer*, anyone within a certain age group will be able to name that tune too.) The melodies in instrumental music, from violin concertos to piano songs, similarly contain recognizable musical phrases that help build the melody as well.

Walks into a Bar

Imagine, for a moment, that your friend Diana has knitted you a scarf. If I ask you what you appreciate about the scarf, you might say that you love the deep blue, royal purple, and teal colors that she's used; the striped pattern; and how she's arranged the stripes so that the purple stands out more than the blue and the teal, since you love to wear purple.

If I ask you what stitch she used to knit the scarf, however, you may not be able to tell me. You don't what particular stitch was used; you just appreciate how the scarf came out! If I ask Diana to look at any knitted garment, on the other hand, she would probably immediately recognize what the stitch pattern was, because the stitch pattern of any knitted garment is immediately obvious to her.

Similarly, in your favorite song, you may be able to pick up the tune and name a few of the back-up instruments. But underlying each song is a specific beat-pattern that may not be immediately recognizable to you, though it is the stitch that holds together the music.

Within any given song, beats are grouped into cycles of a few beats each. Within each cycle, particular beats receive more emphasis than others. Analogously, within each row of stitches in a scarf, some stitches might feature more prominently (and perhaps in a recurring pattern, say, every four stitches) than others. A single cycle within a particular piece of music may consist of three beats, for example; in particular, one strong beat followed by two weaker beats, and this repeated cycle of beats would form the undercurrent for that song.

We can appreciate the end product of these cycles of beats; we might be able to identify a twelve-beat recognizable musical phrase that we fancy, even if we're only subliminally aware of the ongoing pattern of three-beat cycles that underlies it.

The type of stitch we use for a piece of music is called its **meter**. The meter is the particular cycle of beats, and the pattern of emphasis of those beats, used in a song. Each instance of a single cycle of beats is called a **bar**. A bar is analogous to a single small group of scarf-stitches containing particularly prominent and less prominent stitches.

In *Jingle Bells*, for instance, an eight-beat phrase might consist of two-beat cycles, with one strong and one weak beat, thus:

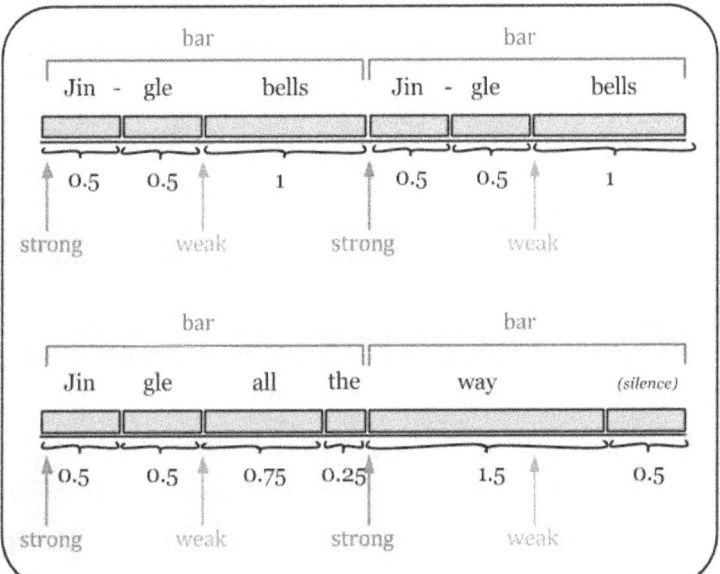

Strong beats are sometimes indicated by accented syllables in the lyrics, louder volume, or a longer note, but in most of the music we listen to, they can still be hard to discern.

It is very common for music to have four-beat cycles. It is less common — though not at all rare — to have a meter with three beats per bar. One example is *Piano Man* by Billy Joel:

Sing us a song, you're the piano man
Sing us a song tonight

This is the rhythm of the first two lines of the chorus, each of which contains twelve beats:

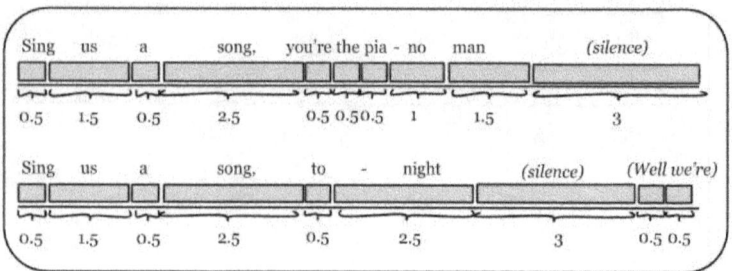

If you were to sway to *Piano Man* (with a tonic and gin in one hand, at a piano bar, of course), you would sway every three beats. This is because the phrases in the song consist of three-beat bars with an emphasis on the first beat of each, as shown below. Your mind might also subconsciously register that, in this case, the harmonies move from chord to chord at the start of each three-beat cycle as well:

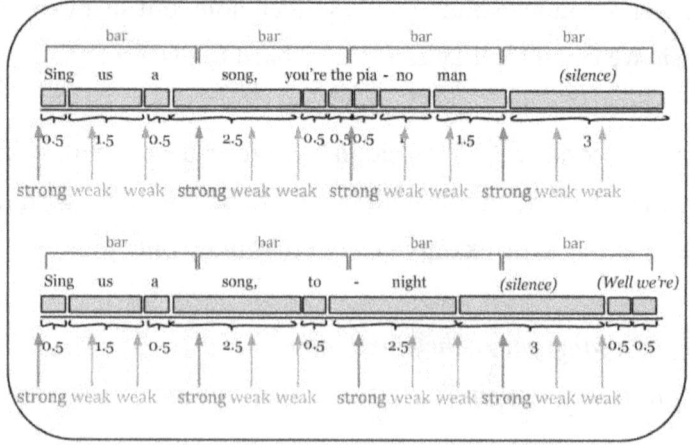

Waltzes famously have three-beat bars, like *Waltz of the Flowers* from The Nutcracker by Pyotr Ilyich Tchaikovsky, and *The Blue Danube* by Richard Strauss. Since this type of music has a lilting feeling, it's also good for putting us to sleep; *Goodnight, My Someone* from *The Music Man* has three-beat bars, as does Johannes Brahms' *Lullaby*.

We've seen a meter with two beats per bar, as well as one with three beats per bar. In addition, it is certainly possible to create meters with cycles of five or seven or other uncommon numbers. *Take 5*, by the jazz group the Dave Brubeck Quartet, famously has five-beat bars, which can be further divided into a group of three beats followed by a group of two beats. The *Mission: Impossible* theme also famously has five-beat bars.

Composers and musicians have also experimented with changing the meter within a given song. In *Hey Ya* by Outkast, every third four-beat bar in the verse is followed by a two-beat bar. *The Sound of Silence* by Simon & Garfunkel also occasionally throws a two-beat bar into a song otherwise consisting of four-beat bars. In *All You Need is Love* by the Beatles, four-beat bars alternate with three-beat bars in the verse.

Don't Worry, Be Happy

Just as we've seen that particular scales and chord progressions can be characteristic of certain types of music, particular rhythms and beat can also be characteristic of certain genres. We already mentioned that waltz is characterized by its three-beat meter; let's now take a look at the rhythms of reggae, as another example.

Reggae typically has four-beat bars, and is characterized in part by a strummed chord on the second half of every beat. We can see how this plays out in the chorus of *One Love*, by Bob Marley. The third line of the chorus is:

Let's get together and feel all right.

Here is the rhythm of this line:

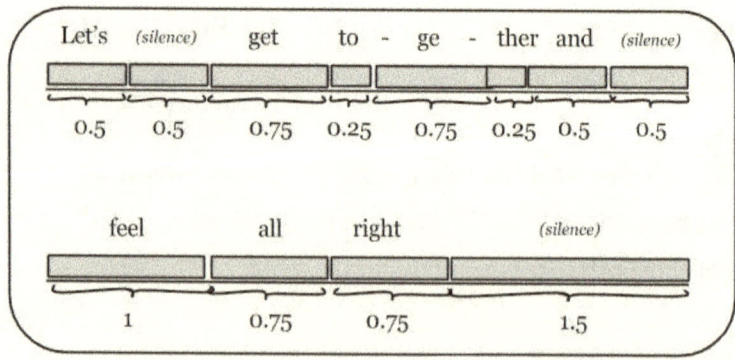

The guitar strums on the second half of each beat, like so:

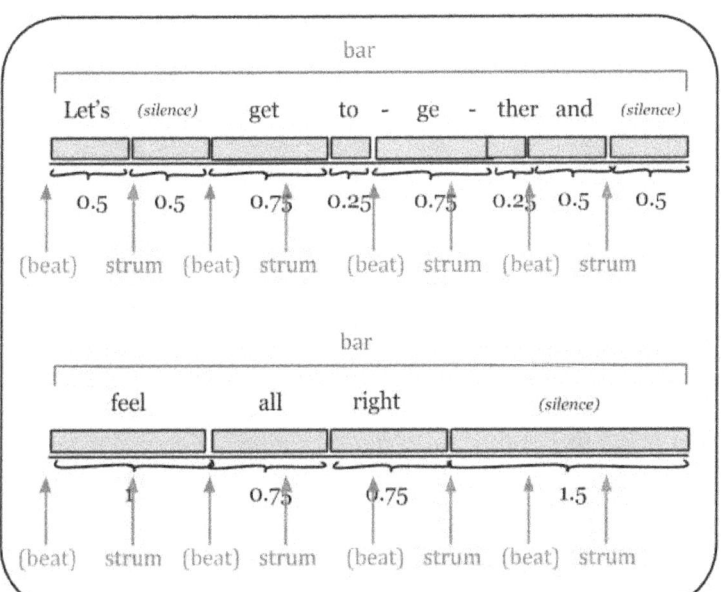

You should be able to hear these distinctive strums on the second half of each beat when you listen to any reggae music.

Rhythm and beat are a curious part of music — without changing a single color in our musical palette, they have a big effect both on the tunes we remember and on the structure underlying our favorite songs. Each instrument's rhythmic patterns lie on top of an underlying pulse, the beat, which is essential to driving a thumping song at a dance club — even if some of us can never seem to find it on the dance floor!

Coda

We hope you've enjoyed this ride through the wonderful world of music. Let's have a quick peek back and see what we learned:

Pitch

Soundwaves are created when an object vibrates and sets off a domino-chain of vibrations that eventually reaches our eardrums and sends signals to our brains. The **frequency** of a soundwave is determined by how many full cycles of the wave hit our ears every second. We measure this in **Hertz** (Hz): one Hz is one full cycle per second. A wave with a higher frequency will sound like it has a higher **pitch**, in the sense of high-pitched voice or the high-pitched shriek of a car alarm. **Notes** are the set of named pitches that we use in our music-making. Amazingly, our brains perceive the difference between soundwaves not according to the absolute difference between frequencies of the waves (e.g. "100 Hz") but according to the **relative** difference between these frequencies (e.g. "1.5 times as high"). Just as physical distance describes the amount of space between two points, an **interval** is the amount of space between two notes. Since only the relative frequencies matter, we need to come up with special "units" to measure intervals that works in terms of relative frequencies. The first key unit for measuring the distance between notes is the **octave**. The octave is the distance between a pitch and the pitch twice or half its frequency. Amazingly, one note and a note that is an octave higher sound like lower and higher version of the same note to our ears. The second key unit for measuring the distance between notes is the **semitone**. A semitone is designed so that there's twelve semitones in an octave. There are thus **twelve notes** used in Western music, which repeat themselves every octave. Seven of the notes are named after the letters *A to G*. The other five commonly have two alternative names; e.g. the note between *A* and *B* can be called $A^\sharp$ (pronounced A-sharp) or $B^\flat$ (pronounced B-flat). Over time, musicians have standardised their notes around a pitch called **Concert A**, sounded at **440 Hz**. We can "pick up and move" a tune so that it starts on any other note; so long as we add or subtract the same number of semitones from every note in the tune we will come out with something that sounds recognisably similar to the original.

Scales

The set of notes that a composer chooses to use in a given piece is called a **scale**. A scale can be any collection of musical notes organised from lowest to highest, but there are special rules that govern all the scales commonly used in Western music. The two most common *types* of scales in Western music are **Major Scales** (which instinctively sound happy to us) and **Minor Scales** (which instinctively sound sad). Every Major Scale follows the same pattern of "hops," just moved up or down the piano. The "simplest" major scale on the piano is C Major, because it only uses the white keys. Musicians have a special language for talking about the general case of the Major Scale: ***Do, Re, Mi, Fa, So, La, Ti, Do.*** The word *Do* becomes a stand-in for whatever note your Major Scale happens to start on, and the other notes follow suit accordingly. While the Major and Minor scale are by far the most common in Western music, there are other types of scales (some of which have differing numbers of notes): Pentatonic Scales, Indian Carnatic Scales, Blues Scales and many others.

Harmony

Most songs we listen to are composed of numerous interlocking **lines**; an individual line is played by a single instrument or sung by a single voice. The most prominent line in a song is called the **melody**, which is often the one sung by the vocalist in a rock or pop song (or one of the instruments if they'd doing a *solo*). It's what we commonly call the "tune." When overlapping lines of music are played at the same time they create **harmony**: the use of simultaneous notes to create particular effects. Some intervals create **consonant** pairings, or pairs of notes that sound good when played simultaneously, and some intervals create

dissonant pairings, or pairs of notes that harsh when played simultaneously. In consonant intervals, the frequencies of the pitches tend to be in simple ratios to each other (such as 3:2). In dissonant intervals, pitches are in complicated ratios to each other (such as 16:15). The interval that is six semitones large is particularly harsh sounding; it was once called the *diabolus in musica*, or "Devil in Music." Every interval has an **inversion** where the notes "flip" positions, with the bottom one going on top. For example, if we start by playing an *A* and the *C* just above it, the inversion would be playing that same *C* with the *A* just above it. An interval and its inversion add up to twelve semitones. A group of three or more notes played simultaneously is called a **chord**. If we put three notes together in such a way that the intervals between all the pairs in the chord are consonant, the chord itself will also sound pleasing. A chord (with three notes) built on an interval of *four* semitones beneath an interval of *three* semitones sounds qualitatively happy, and we call it a **major chord**. A chord (with three notes) built on an interval of *three* semitones beneath an interval of *four* semitones sounds qualitatively sad, and we call it a **minor chord**. If we play four (or more) notes simultaneously, we necessarily introduce some dissonance between at least two of those notes. These four-note chords have a variety of interesting qualities. Within any given scale, we can build a chord beginning on each note of the scale. The chord beginning on the seventh note of the Major Scale is neither major nor minor, because it has an interval of *three* semitones beneath an interval of *three* semitones. We call this a **diminished chord**. Chords are named with Roman numerals according to the scale they're in and whether they're major or minor. The chord starting on the first note of a scale will be named *I* if it is a major chord and *i* if it is a minor chord; subsequent chords will be named *II* or *ii*, then *III* or *iii*, then *IV* or *iv*, etc. The diminished chord starting on the seventh note of the Major Scale is named *vii°*. A **chord progression** is a sequence of chords that often underlies a melody. A chord progression will often start on the first note of the scale that we're working in, wander away from it, and then move back towards it again over some stretch of time. Musical **tension** is the feeling that a particular chord in a progression is unstable, and so a bad place for the music to stop; **resolution** is the feeling that a particular chord in a progression is stable and so is a reasonable place for the music to pause or end. Many rock and pop tunes can be composed using just four chords: *I, IV, V, vi*.

Rhythm & Beat

In any given tune, not all notes are of equal duration. **Rhythm** is the pattern of duration of notes (and silences) in a particular line of music. Every piece of music has a **beat**, a basic pulse that underlies the music. The **tempo** is the speed at which a song is played. Tempo is measured in beats per minute. A **phrase** is a piece of music with a distinct, discernible musical shape, typically spanning a line or two of lyrics in popular music. The **meter** is the particular cycle of beats, and the pattern of emphasis of those beats, used in a song. Each instance of a single cycle of beats is called a **bar**. Songs most commonly use a meter consisting of four beats. Reggae is characterized by a four-beat meter, with a chord sounded on the second half of each beat. Meters consisting of three beats per measure create a lilting feeling. Waltzes have a three-beat meter.

And that's that! We've covered a lot of ground in a few short pages, but there's still so much left to say and learn. Now that we've dipped our toes in the big ideas behind music, we hope you'll want to dive in and keep swimming. Maybe, if we're lucky, we'll even get the chance to make music together some day. Wherever you hear a beautiful harmony or a toe-tapping beat, that's where we'll be (not literally, of course, because that would be weird). Thanks for reading!

Thinking Musically Coda

THINKING MUSICALLY

ANUPAMA PATTABIRAMAN & URI BRAM

Capara Books

This book would not have been possible without the help and inspiration of family and friends.

Anu and Uri would like to express their unending indebtedness to…

the 55 people who backed our Kickstarter, and set us off on the road to this book:

Mohammed Taher	Jiashuo Feng
KifKaf	Anand Pattabiraman
Eric Schlossberg	Bryan Locascio
Keisuke Ishihara	Aditya Panda
Katie Camille	Emily Silk
TeraTelnet	Kelly Lack
Stephen	Parinda Wanitwat
Michael Lemma	Sara Shaw
Talia Billig	Julia
C G P	Uma Santhanam
Deborah Chang	Paul Ginart
LRG	Scott Blake
Kalid Azad	Rodger Boots
Adam Ernst	Kejia Tang
Lily Cheng	Andrew Sue-Ako
Tyro Prate	Vigneshwaran
Bruce Cichowlas	Carlton Frost
Janice Chou	Daniel Echelman
Diana Chien	Meredith Bock
Maya Kherani	Jason Chua
Yaffa Fredrick	Ben Smith
Erica Zendell	Gayatri Muthukrishnan
Thomas Dallan	Jyothishmathi Swaminathan
Andrew Bogorad	Shanthi Subramanian
Taotao Liu	Ramamoorthy Subramanian
Jonathan Giuffrida	and Subramanian Muthukrishnan.

Thank you all from the bottom of our hearts, your faith and support have meant the world to us;

and to Tiffany Lu, conductor extraordinaire, and the greatest editor a book could wish for.

On a personal note, Anu would like to express immense gratitude to...

Amma and to her family, for encouraging her to entertain wild ideas;

to Emily and Eddie, for lending our drafts their eyes and brains;

to the friends she's made through music, for allowing her to use movable Do;

and to her music teachers, for their neverending wisdom, and for teaching her to count to four.

Uri would like to send a most heartfelt "thank you" to...

Melanie and Gil, for laughter and encouragement in the early days of the book;

to Mari and Mark, for the perfect artist's loft as the book was wrapping up;

to Kalid, of MAKS fame, for understanding everything;

and to Xin, for finger piano on the subway, and catching the last/first ride.

Last but not least, Anu and Uri would like to thank you, dear reader, for coming on this adventure with us. We hope you enjoyed it, and we'd love to hear from you! While Uri wanders the world, Anu can pretty solidly be found in the United States, particularly in the Northeast. You can even more easily find us at thinkingmusically.com, or by closing your eyes and tapping your heels three times and thinking of music.

About the Authors

Anu Pattabiraman. Main Instruments: Voice, Cello

Anu has been singing, playing cello, and dabbling with numerous other instruments since the age of 4. She has been trained in classical Indian music, sung opera, and performed in orchestras. Anu has made numerous appearances with choirs across the world, performing at Notre Dame Cathedral in Paris, St. Mark's Basilica in Venice, and at Washington, D.C.'s Kennedy Center alongside the National Symphony Orchestra.

Uri Bram. Main Instruments: Pen, Paper

Uri's first book, *Thinking Statistically,* made key statistical concepts fun and accessible for a statsphobic audience - it has been rated as one of the 99 best business books ever written by NYT bestselling author Josh Kaufman, and been featured on reading lists at top universities across the world. Uri loves making intimidating topics easy to understand for curious, intelligent people.

www.ingramcontent.com/pod-product-compliance
Lightning Source LLC
LaVergne TN
LVHW090116080426
835507LV00040B/912